THE PATCH THEOREM
A Philosophy of Death, Life and Time

CHARLES MWEWA

Published by:

AFRICA IN CANADA PRESS

Ottawa, Ontario

Canada

Copyright © 2022 Charles Mwewa

All rights reserved.

ISBN: 978-1-988251-41-7

DEDICATION

For us,

Because we will all meet death someday.

CONTENTS

DEDICATION iii
CONTENTS v
PREFACE vii
1 | DEATH AND LIFE AND TIME 1
    Chapter Content 1
    The Nature of Death and Dying 1
    The Wisdom of Living Right 3
    Life is a Gift, Death an Investment 13
    Theorem of Death and Life 26
    Breath of Life Exchange (BOLE) 33
    Time 38
    Stages of Death 54
    The Human Trinity 77
    The Poetry of Creation 84
    Judgment in the Context of 90
    First and Second Deaths 90
    Conclusion 105
REVIEW QUESTIONS 109
2 | THE PATCH 119
    Chapter Content 119

- The Soul's Delicate Design 119
  - (1) The Subconscious Patch 121
    - From Pre-birth to Birth 122
    - Dependent Stage 122
    - The Milk Stage of Life 123
    - Pleasure-seeking Development Stage 125
  - (2) The Subcortical Patch 128
    - Emotional Restructuring Experience 128
    - Truth-in-Emotions 129
    - The Resolution 130
    - The Equilibrium 131
    - Assumptions of the Subcortical Patch 132
  - (3) The Subphemeral Patch 133
    - Subphemeral Consciousness 134
    - Subphemeral Deconfrigration 135
    - Subphemeral Resolution 135
  - Conclusion 137
- REVIEW QUESTIONS 139
- ABOUT THE AUTHOR 147
- INDEX 149

PREFACE

All humans at some point have asked three questions: Who am I? Where did I come from? And Where am I going? These questions have tended to be addressed through theories, such as the Evolution Theory or the Creationist Theory. However, these two theories have also tended to raise unanswered questions. At one end, the Evolution Theory is overtly scientific and is not universally accepted. The Creationist Theory tends to be religious in nature and those from the philosophical and scientific backgrounds are inclined to consider it as overtly oversimplified. In the middle, are those who believe in both – tending to fill the gaps left by the Creationist Theory with the Evolution Theory.

As such, behavior is predicated upon one's belief in life, death and the after-life. Those who are scientific in their postulations, emphasize the present and the now. To them, life is what you make it now. To them, death may be the end of everything or the beginning of another dimensional recreation (reincarnation). For those who believe in the Creationist Theory, life, death and the after-life have an eternal relationship. What one did and does in this life is as much part of their life and death cycle. So, there is resurrection and judgment, and the continuation of living after that.

In the *Patch Theorem: A Philosophy of Death, Life and Time*, the author introduces a third dimension (trimention) of explaining birth, death, life (and even life after death) and time. The elements of the Creationist Theory are recognized, and the postulations of science are affirmed. However, both religion and science cannot explain life and death from the realist point of view. The creation or experience called humanity is trimentional; it exists at the subconscious, subcortical and subphemeral layers.

These layers correspond to pre-birth, birth and the borderline within the post-death existence of a human being. And to complete this, humans have a trinity of structure: They are a body, a soul (mind) and a spirit. In the theory of evolution by natural selection, Charles Darwin and Alfred Russel Wallace could not explain where nature itself originated from. They were able to observe and explain nature, but they did not understand how nature evolved or came about. Moses, on the other hand, believed that the world was created by the Word of God. Although the Mosaic Theory cannot be explained empirically, it has tremendous credibility when it comes to every-day experience of life and death. Indeed, where the Mosaic postulations leave gaps, such as "God said let there be…and there was," the Evolution Theory tends to provide, to some degree of details, the experimental process that might have given rise to the result. In this regard, therefore, both theories have provided some level of understanding of creation.

That said, the *Patch Theorem: A Philosophy of Death, Life and Time*, is not meant to be a theory of creation. It is the attendant observation (using both spiritual and philosophical observations) of the experience of life and death. Hitherto, only Jesus Christ can be said to have been the only human being who was born, lived, died and rose again to tell humanity the organization of the physical and metaphysical worlds. And, therefore, Jesus, more than Muhammad, Confucius or Buddha, or the Greek philosophers, has more credibility because He experienced all the realms. We can ignore his postulations to our own detriment, no matter how irreligious we may be. However, the rest of what Jesus did not tell or say, can only be explained or inferred through the tools of experiential observation, faith and a little bit of reason.

In the *Patch Theorem: A Philosophy of Death, Life and Time*, experiential observation and faith marry to produce a philosophical explanation of life, death, time and the after-life. Happiness, therefore, rests on the preparation one makes while living in a live body. This preparation started with a Knowledge Acquisition Device (or KAD) and is intrinsically provided by the subconscious device which reads the end clock and grants every human being the awareness possible before they breathe their last. Humans may be social animals, but when it comes to life and death, they are not born without an inherent plan and a predetermined end unlike animals – the beginning of the after-life. Their natural internal clock does all and everything to prepare them for life and death – and life after.

The book begins by providing a theory of death, life and time, before delving into the rudiments of the internal temporal alarm clock which leads to the eternal divine expiration. The theoretical foundation is necessary to provide an inter-sectorial analysis of the forces that may be at play in the human experience of birth, life, death, time and a glimpse of the after-life. Like sleep itself, everyone will experience death or rapture at some point, so it is in order for us to discuss both.

cm.

1 | DEATH AND LIFE AND TIME

Chapter Content

The Nature of Death and Dying
The Wisdom of Living Right
Human Problem, Divine Solution
Life is a Gift, Death an Investment
Theorem of Death and Life
Time
Stages of Death
The Human Trinity
The Poetry of Creation
Judgment in the Context of First and Second Deaths
Conclusion

The Nature of Death and Dying

When you have a clear view of death, you have a clear view of life. Think of death this way, it is the last rite every human must undergo before a new and better world is formed. Death doesn't end anything; it merely begins a full life dispensation. Death will come to anything that has been born, the question is not when; the real question is what? What one does while they are alive is the determining factor of what they will receive or become after death. When one fully understands that one day they will die, they also know that now is the time to do good. Dying is not about quantity, it is more about quality; whether one died young or old, depends on what values they embraced and the service they rendered.

Birth is important to death. There cannot be death without birth. Everything that is born will die. Birth is not an indication that death will pass, it is a sign that life will continue. What does it then mean to die? Among others, death is a giant sleep, except that it is one in which all dreams may be suspended. In that regard, death is an equalizer; millennia, epochs, eras, centennials, decades, years, months, weeks, days or seconds, do not count.

There is a co-relationship between how death happens and how we fall asleep. We all know that we will sleep. We may even consciously prepare to go to bed and sleep. We know we will sleep, but at what point, we do not know. It is enough, through sheer experience, to know that we will sleep. The "how" of sleep is a secret of nature and its Creator. So is death. It happens in a twinkling of an eye, and so will be resurrection. Thus, the irony about death is that everyone who encounters it will recognize it, albeit very briefly. Just like we recognize that we are falling asleep, then everything is suspended thereafter, save for dreaming, so it is with death.

The Wisdom of Living Right

When we die, this life ends, and another will begin at some point later, for good or for bad. Unlike in life, in death we achieve absolute refinement. This refinement has to do with the body and the soul. The spirit in man does not die. In death, it returns to its Creator and the soul is suspended. The body, though, decays and returns to the soil. Therefore, anything that is called a body, has a definite lifespan because it exists within time. Everybody would have a grave or a place where their bodies last remained.

From the earthly point of view, death has three benefits: Rest to the body; fertilization; and regeneration. The body eventually ages and must be retired. Death gives it that necessary rest. As it is buried, the body offers additional fertilization to the earth, just like when plants die and decay, they become manure to perpetuate the existence of the earth. In that regard as well, this earth is permanent. It was created once and it will not be created again. The "new" earth will be the old earth renewed, and that will happen after Judgment Day. Those who will return to live on the "new" earth, would have first died or have been raptured and experienced resurrection. Then they will live on the "new" earth in new bodies forever. The souls of those who will not survive Judgment Day will be lost in Hell.

Death and life are an accounting system, at some point, we will be called upon to give account. The caveat is that all the balances must happen before the person tastes death or is raptured. After death, there may be no reconciliation. One should, therefore, live their lives daily as if today they will die, because they may.

The greatness of anyone who is alive, will be revealed after they have been dead. The life they lived before they died, will best be judged after they are dead. However good one is to the dead; the dead cannot appreciate anything. Therefore, if one has to be good, they must be good to the living. In short, only the living are capable of saying, "Thank you!"

THE PATCH THEOREM

Death is the temporary stoppage to life's dream line, and literally, the permanent stoppage of sleep-dreaming. In the former, all plans come to an end. In death, law is suspended and visions can no longer be fulfilled. Before death, there is no judgment. Lack of vision gives death an easy ride. Thus, "…in the end, there is nothing left to pass on to one's children. We all come to the end of our lives as naked and empty-handed as on the day we were born. We can't take our riches with us. And this, too, is a very serious problem. People leave this world no better off than when they came. All their hard work is for nothing—like working for the wind. Throughout their lives, they live under a cloud—frustrated, discouraged, and angry."[1]

The wisdom of living is, therefore, in this respect, that when death comes, you should have your account in order. It is easier for every do-gooder to say and do good things when they are dying than when they have life. Fear of death, particularly, fear of the unknown destination, causes some people to want to do and say good before they die. However, death usually comes like a thief in the night.[2] Both life

---

[1] Ecclesiastes 5:8ff; Song of Solomon 8:14ff
[2] See also Revelation 16:15, Matthew 24:43, 1 Thessalonians 5:2, 1 Thessalonians 5:4, 2 Peter 3:10

and death are important; in life one should occupy, in death one may know and remember nothing, and in the after-life, one will have to give an account of how they lived their lives. An investor urged his servants to "Occupy till I come."[3] Islam has a similar view:

> …death is not an end to our existence; it is a passage, which takes us from this world to the hereafter – the actual purpose for our creation and the result of our work in this life. Whether we fear death or not depends on how much we have prepared for the reckoning of the Day of Judgment. Preparing for death is a lifetime's job. It begins on the day you reach the age of *bulugh* and are held accountable for your deeds in the eyes of Almighty Allah.[4]

For those people who follow the teachings of Confucius, the injunction is to live a moral upright life before one dies. They must display propriety, filial piety, appropriateness, and humanness, and this stand should be

---

[3] Luke 19:13
[4] Sayyid Muhammad Rizvi, "What You Should Do Just before Death," https://www.al-islam.org/articles/what-you-should-do-just-death-sayyid-muhammad-rizvi accessed on July 16th, 2022

continuous even in the last moment of life.[5] To die right, one must have lived right.

Human Problem, Divine Solution

Death is a human problem, but a divine solution. Death leaves behind more problems than it takes. It silences everything, except what is written or recorded. Death, is a long silence: "The dead do not praise the Lord, nor do any who go down into silence."[6] Wisdom here is that, we should praise the Lord while we have breath. We should make a holy noise while we live: "Make a joyful noise to the Lord, all the earth; break forth into joyous song and sing praises!"[7]

The weakness of death is that, it can't kill the soul, and it can't end life permanently. Life will go on after the resurrection. However, the strength of death is that it comes like a thief in the night, and sometimes it may catch one just when they are in their prime.

---

[5] Chiung-Yin Hsu, Margaret O'Connor & Susan Lee (2009) Understandings of Death and Dying for People of Chinese Origin, Death Studies, 33:2, 153-174, DOI: 10.1080/07481180802440431 (emphasis added)
[6] Psalm 115:17
[7] Psalm 98:4; see also Psalm 6:5

To those who believe in Jesus Christ and do good in Christianity, death may be a nice, uninterrupted sleep, waking up into eternal bliss and splendor. For Muslims, beliefs in Judgment Day and the after-life inspire them to live right before death and to seek for forgiveness from both men (and women) and God. In Buddhism, the idea of *Karma* inspires good and sincere living: "According to Buddhism, everything that happens is the result of *Karma* – the law of cause and effect. Every action throughout a person's lifetime, both good and bad, has an effect on their future. The way a person lives his or her life also affects the way they die. So, it is very important for a Buddhist to prepare for death by living in a good and kind manner."[8]

Accordingly, when death comes, one should be sure that they have been saved (Christians), have lived a life of piety (Confucius) and have lived life in a good and kind manner (Buddhism). The death alarm rings at varying times for different people; the resurrection alarm may ring at the same time for all. For Christians, death was once a vicious monster

---

[8] "Buddhist Funeral Traditions," <https://www.alexander-levittfunerals.com/download/13534/BuddhistFuneralT.pdf> accessed on July 16th, 2022

which Jesus tamed into a wagon transporting people to their respective eternal destinations. And in terms of everlasting rewards, death is neutral; all it does, after judgment, is giving one a passage into Heaven or into Hell.

Christians believe that death has never defeated anyone who died in Christ. For death to have a lethal bite, those it kills must not regain life. This is possible only if death can also prevent resurrection or reincarnation. Christianity gives a very powerful revelation of how death lost its grip: "O Death, where is your sting? O Hades, where is your victory? The sting of death is sin, and the strength of sin is the law. But thanks be to God, who gives us the victory through our Lord Jesus Christ."[9]

Death and Hades are two sides of the same coin. The inference here is that before Christ, death would give a bite and Hades would lock up the culprit. Thus, the idea of being dead forever was solidified. Both death's sting (sin) and its strength (the law) were eliminated through Jesus Christ. Jesus came and took "away our sins. And in him is no sin,"[10] and Peter confirms, thus, "He himself bore our sins

---

[9] 1 Corinthians 15:55-57
[10] 1 John 3:5

in his body on the cross, so that we might die to sins and live for righteousness; 'by his wounds you have been healed.'"[11] Both death and illness were dealt with in Jesus' body. This effectively took away the sting of death. And then Jesus Christ ended the law, "For Christ is the end of the law for righteousness to everyone who believes."[12] Thus, the sting (sin) of death and its strength (law) were taken away in Christ. And God lowered the threshold for escaping the permanency of death, it is called grace. People are saved by a simple faith in Jesus Christ. Neither performances nor elaborate liturgies are necessary for salvation.[13]

For Christians, this argument means two things. First, that grace has overpowered death. This claim establishes the foundation for faith, life and death. No matter how and where death occurs, those who believe in Jesus Christ are safe in Him. And second, that death is a mere formality, or a passage into glory. It is as Joseph once said, "You intended to harm me, but God intended it for good to accomplish what is now being done, the saving of many lives."[14] This

---

[11] 1 Peter 2:24
[12] Romans 10:4
[13] See Ephesians 2:2-9
[14] Genesis 50:20

amazing power of God was proclaimed in a doxology by Apostle Paul, thus, "Now to Him who is able to do exceedingly abundantly above all that we ask or think, according to the power that works in us, to Him be glory in the church by Christ Jesus to all generations, forever and ever. Amen."[15]

To defeat death, according to Christian doctrine, one has to defeat sin and its twin side, Hades. Since no human being can defeat sin and Hades, one has to rely upon the One who did defeat sin and Hades, the Man, Jesus Christ. It is a simple formula. Thus, if one is saved, or has served God and humanity with sincerity, or has seen their grand children, one can be ready to be transported into their rest awaiting the resurrection of the dead.

Both humans and Satan are only capable of killing the human body, but they can't kill the soul. God, however, can kill both the human body and its soul: "Do not be afraid of those who kill the body but cannot kill the soul. Rather, be afraid of the One who can destroy both soul and body in Hell."[16] Implicitly, this injunction demands that one fears no death at

---
[15] See Ephesians 3:20
[16] Matthew 10:28

all, but should fear God and should fear living a life without purpose. The way one treats others before they die, is likely to be the way they will be treated when they die. If one was good to others, those others will likely treat them well and with respect and dignity in death.

The death assignment will end after it has met many human beings; some appointments will be interrupted by the rapture (the transporting of believers to Heaven at the Second Coming of Christ). However, death will eventually die. Indeed, we are escorted to the gates of eternity by death, and by the same token, welcomed, after the resurrection, by Eternal Life.

The longer one lived on earth is only important if one lived it meaningfully. It is, however, a liability to live a long and fruitless life. Despite that, only God must decide when one's life ends. A long life is no longer a mark of righteousness; it is, partly, a sign of maintaining good hygiene, paying attention to hazards, and sheer luck. Both prayer and medicine have the power to postpone death. Death and life are a joint-venture between God and humans, both have a say. It is better, though, to die early and young in righteousness, than to live a long life in unrighteousness. It is ultimately the best to die both in old age and in righteousness.

Life is a Gift, Death an Investment

Life makes living a gift, death makes it an investment. This dichotomic realization implies that one must treasure the gift and account for the investment. All religions recognize this fact, that the Creator will require an account of how we lived our lives. In that regard, life is a gift with instructions on how we should live it. Those instructions come within the design of our conscience. Therefore, we might have not chosen our birth, but in life, we should be grateful, and in death, we should account for life.

There seems to be four states of death. Death is an act; it is a process; it is a state; and it is a personality. The Christian Bible brings out the four states very succinctly.

As an act, we read in Genesis: "Now Cain said to his brother Abel, 'Let's go out to the field.' While they were in the field, Cain attacked his brother Abel and *killed* him."[17]

---

[17] Genesis 4:8 (emphasis added)

As a process, death can be triggered, such as through taking chemical poisons, molesting the body or through plans of vengeance. In Exodus, God commands, "You shall not murder."[18]

As a state, according to the Bible, by faith, Christians are already dead; they died with Christ in baptism: "Or are you ignorant that as many as have been baptized into Christ Jesus have been baptized into His death? We have been buried therefore with Him through baptism into death."[19]

In principle, Christians, by the time of the resurrection, would have died twice – thus, will not be hurt by the second death. This is clearly and convincingly stated in Revelation: "…those who overcome the devil's tribulation have part in the first resurrection and will not be hurt by the second death, which has no power over them."[20] The way to avoid the second death is to take part in the second death, vicariously, through faith in Jesus Christ.

---

[18] Exodus 20:13; see also 1 Corinthians 6:19-20; Romans 12:19;
[19] Romans 6:3-4
[20] Revelation 2:11 and 20:6

And as a personality, death is called an enemy: "The last enemy to be destroyed is death."[21] And this makes sense in the context of Hebrews 9:27. For if it has been appointed for men to die once and after that judgment, and if after judgment unbelievers would have to be thrown into the Lake of Fire (the second death), then death must be destroyed last.

The destruction of death will entail the sanctioning of the new regime of everlasting life – and "He will wipe every tear from their eyes. There will be no more death or mourning or crying or pain, for the old order of things has passed away."[22] And that "new order of things," may, graciously, be based right here on earth: "And I John saw the holy city, new Jerusalem, coming down from God *out of heaven*, prepared as a bride adorned for her husband. And I heard a great voice out of heaven saying, Behold, the tabernacle of *God is with men*, and *he will dwell with them, and they shall be his people, and God himself shall be with them, and be their God.* And he that sat upon the throne said, Behold, *I make all things new.* And he said

---

[21] 1 Corinthians 15:26
[22] Revelation 21:4

unto me, Write: for these words are true and faithful."[23]

Only God has the power to give and to take a life: "See now that I, even I, am He, and there is no god besides Me. I kill, and I make alive; I wound, and I heal; neither is there any that can deliver out of My hand."[24] Satan can take life (can kill), but he cannot create life: "The thief [Satan] comes only to steal and kill and destroy; I have come that they may have life, and have it to the full."[25] This fact was clearly demonstrated in the confrontation between Moses and Pharaoh.

Moses turned water into blood, "But the magicians of Egypt did the same by their secret arts."[26]

Moses plagued all of Egypt with frogs, "But the magicians did the same by their secret arts and made frogs come up on the land of Egypt."[27]

Moses turned the dust of the earth into gnats in all the land of Egypt. "The magicians tried

---

[23] Revelation 21:2-3, 5 (emphasis is added).
[24] Deuteronomy 32:39
[25] John 10:10
[26] Exodus 7:22
[27] Exodus 8:7

by their secret arts to produce gnats, but they could not. So, there were gnats on man and beast. Then the magicians said to Pharaoh, 'This is the finger of God.' But Pharaoh's heart was hardened, and he would not listen to them, as the Lord had said."[28]

Moses sent swarms of flies in Egypt and on Pharaoh's servants and his people, and into their houses. "But Pharaoh hardened his heart this time also, and did not let the people go."[29]

Moses caused severe plague to fall upon the livestock that were in the field, the horses, the donkeys, the camels, the herds, and the flocks. "But the heart of Pharaoh was hardened, and he did not let the people go."[30]

Moses brought boils upon Egypt, "And the magicians could not stand before Moses because of the boils, for the boils came upon the magicians and upon all the Egyptians. But the Lord hardened the heart of Pharaoh, and he did not listen to them, as the Lord had spoken to Moses."[31]

---

[28] Exodus 8:16
[29] Exodus 8: 32
[30] Exodus 9:7
[31] Exodus 9:11-12

Moses caused very heavy hail to fall, such as never had been in Egypt from the day it was founded until then. "But when Pharaoh saw that the rain and the hail and the thunder had ceased, he sinned yet again and hardened his heart, he and his servants."[32]

Moses brought forth locusts, "But the Lord hardened Pharaoh's heart, and he did not let the people of Israel go."[33]

Moses brought in darkness, "But the Lord hardened Pharaoh's heart, and he would not let them go."[34]

Then finally, God killed the first born of every Egyptian, including Pharaoh's heir apparent. "Then [Pharaoh] summoned Moses and Aaron by night and said, 'Up, go out from among my people, both you and the people of Israel; and go, serve the Lord, as you have said. Take your flocks and your herds, as you have said, and be gone, and bless me also!'"[35]

---

[32] Exodus 9:34
[33] Exodus 10:20
[34] *Ibid.*, verse 27
[35] Exodus 12:31-32

In total, there were ten plagues that God, through Moses, brought upon Egypt. Only the plague of death finally got the stubborn Pharaoh to surrender. Satan, through Pharaoh's magicians, could certainly perform some trivial miracles, and even create some animal life. Satan could kill, including killing human life. But Satan is unable to create human life. God unleashed death upon Egypt, but death could not violate the blood covenant the people had with God in the Passover. Blood kept death away from God's people.

And the lessons here are three: First, that only God can both create and kill human beings. Second, that death can only take what God permits. And third, that death (God's enemy) has a purpose in God's eternal scheme. God has death on a leash, and only lets him loose to accomplish God's divine plan. The end is to have those who will not be raptured taste death, rise, then face judgment. After that, death will be destroyed, ushering in a "new order of things."

God has both the right and the power to kill human life, humans do not have that right. The reason why death will be killed (thrown into the Lake of Fire) is because it murders or kills.

Thus, if a human commits murder, like death, their destiny is the Lake of Fire. Similarly, suicide is an act of self-murder, which, of necessity, would attract the same punishment.

Suicide, under this theory, for whatever reason, is not justified. Abortion is proscribed for the same reason. The criteria is, thus, set according to the three elements of life – the presence of the breath of life; knowledge; and memory. Anyone who is breathing, has knowledge or memory is not subject to be killed by another human being. Babies (including the unborn) have breath in them; those on a life-assisted machines may still have knowledge and memory in them. And any other combination of these, and so long as one of these elements is present, humans are forbidden from arbitrarily meting out death.

In terms of suicide, all the elements of life are present: Breath, knowledge and memory. In fact, it may be argued, that the person contemplating suicide would have known or remembered something traumatic that could be the cause of the anticipated suicide. The aim of this work is not to dispute motivation or the prevailing social or psychological factors that might have triggered suicide. It does not offer a legal framework under which the acceptance of suicide may be viewed, either. In as far as death is concerned, suicide is the termination of the human life. And since only God has the right and power to eliminate life, suicide may be regarded as murder.

In terms of abortion, if it is accepted that the fetus engages in the breath of life (it breathes), then it can be construed that it is in possession of the faculties of life. Indeed, a fetus does not know and it can't remember, either. However, it can breathe.

Terminating a pregnancy by means of abortion may conveniently be considered ending a life. Whether abortion is murder or infanticide depends on many factors, such as the condition of the pregnancy, the health implication of the mother and the child, medical history and etc. The rule is: If saving the child will kill the mother, and if saving the mother will kill the child, abortion may be justified. However, if saving both would lead to birth defects or disability, both must be saved. The caveat is, when in doubt, attempt to save both. And, of course, some may argue, why not invoking the author of life to intervene by way of a miracle and save both?

When it comes to insurance, death is as costly as life. The cost of death is justified, because we loved them and they are no longer with us. It is a wonderful send off to the after-life, although the dead are incapable of appreciating the gesture.

However, the following principles must motivate the living to honor the dead: We bury the dead with the soil of good memories and water them with tears of love. Those who will not fear one's dead body, are the ones who loved them unconditionally, if they did not fear it for monetary gain. Death must be a clarion to the living, that they should be dead to sin, but be alive to righteousness.

The cemetery is the most harmless and the safest place on earth, if human machinations don't intervene. Therefore, it is one's responsibility to honor their living body; but it is others' responsibility to honor the dead body, while it is God's prerogative to take care of the soul.

The dead will be most remembered if they loved others, remembered moderately if they served others, and remembered least if they hated and demeaned others. We must all remember to remember the dead; death has no monopoly on memories. And we should not despise a dead human body, for its Creator may bring us to account.

It is better to mourn than laugh at the funeral of another, because the true end of anyone is the secret that only God holds. One of the most important reasons why we mourn the dead is so that we don't forget that when they lived, they were just like us. And we must bury the dead with the soil of good memories and water them with tears of love.

The idea of dying should motivate us to explore within our temporal limits the wealth of potential and abilities deposited in us by divine providence. For no generation is superior to, or more honored than, another; when we shall all wake up in the new world, we should give account of what and how we invested our gifts while on earth. Because death shall happen, it is incumbent upon us to do all and everything to rise in rank, stand out or gain any available earthly trophies while alive. Indeed, every human alive has a divine contract to subdue the earth and expand the brain. And on that contract, we must perform our part, and God His part.

Before death, we must give all our best, our dearest and our strongest. Death should find us empty – empty of creativity, ideas and innovations – because we should give it all before we die. Death rarely succeeds in its first attempt at taking those who live with a perpetual vision. When we understand that we are valuable and important to another person on earth, it should motivate us to live healthier, steadier, more careful and a bit longer. The will of God for our lives and fate keep us alive even in the face of imminent death.

Death will come, but we should not let it take us before we fulfil our purposes here on earth. "Now when David had served God's purpose in his own generation, he fell asleep; he was buried with his ancestors and his body decayed."[36] Only God has lived throughout all generations. Humans are limited to their own generations. Each person has a duty to their generation. Once their time passes, God will bring in others to fulfil His purposes through those other people. We, therefore, do not do God a favor when we serve His purpose, we

---

[36] Acts 13:36

do our time, and we retire through death. Everyone must discover what their purpose is in their generation, and devote all their time, energy and resources to fulfilling it in their own generation. We will take nothing out of the earth, but we can leave having fulfilled our purposes.

A fool is a person whom God had given wealth or time or abilities or talents or resources or opportunities but they chose to abuse such or misuse such for their own earthly glory. Such people would have left the earth without any investments in the world to come.[37] Wisdom demands that we are grateful to God, loving to others and caring for our earth. When time is up, it's time to go, and it's for others to take over.

At some point, even death must postpone its mission if we are determined to add to our years fruit and character. We should live our lives as if we have once survived death. Death is good only if it signifies one's completion of the earthly mission. If it cuts short our mission, then that is a bad death. Before death, we should redeem the past, maximize the present and have faith in the future. For even death

---

[37] See also Matthew 6:19–20

itself, is God's servant; it gathers and records, for God, generations past, present and future.

Theorem of Death and Life

The mystery of life and death is as simple and complex as to form (substance) and function, as to body and spirit, and as to what comes first, an egg or a chicken, knowledge or memory, light or darkness, and death or life.

If in the beginning there was darkness, then light had preceded darkness, for it is only by the knowledge that there was light that darkness could be perceived and idealized.

Life can exist while there is darkness and darkness can exist while there is light but the human faculties can decide which one to perceive. Thus, the presence of light does not prove the absence of darkness and the presence of darkness does not prove the absence of light, but each solidifies the perception of the other.

When babies are formed, they are alive, and when they are born, they may be alive or dead – alive because the vital signs of life are present and dead if the vital signs of life are absent.

Every live baby is only alive by virtue of breathing, although it neither knows nor remembers anything, just like when people die, we may infer that they neither know nor remember.

The question is: What comes first, death or life? Some would say death because despite being formed, the body is dead unless it is infused with the spirit of life. Others would surmise it is life, because from whence we progress to our death. However, just as the question: What comes first, an egg or the chicken? cannot be answered in the affirmative with one, eliminating the other, so it is with life and death.

What is apparent, therefore, is the recourse to form (substance) and function. For all intentions and purposes, the form (body) is dead *ab initio* until the spirit gives it life. In this sequence, the form is first and the function is second. When they die, the spirit goes first, leaving the flesh to decay back to its pre-formation stage of matter, just like in the beginning the form was dead until the spirit of life entered it and it became a living soul.

The dichotomy set in Genesis 1:2 is illustrative of this fact: "Now the earth was formless and empty, darkness was over the surface of the deep." Prior, in Genesis 1:2, God had made them both, the heavens and the earth. The earth was there, but without life, only formless, empty and dark.

Formless, emptiness and darkness explain the state of death. God's Word (Spirit) regenerated the dead earth and gave it life. In that regard, as it pertains to earth and human formation, death precedes life, but at the same time, life had already existed through its progenitor, who is the Creator God.

So, if the breath of life and light are removed from the earth, it would return to its original state – formless, empty, and dark. But it cannot be denied that the so-called dead earth has potential for being alive well imbedded into its structures. Thus, when light is added, it can spring into life – bearing all sorts of plants and animals and supporting them with water and nutrients. The breath of life causes the dead earth to spring into life.

The human being behaves in the similar fashion. Its material nature (body) is born with what may be called the Knowledge Acquisition Device (or KAD). KAD is embedded within it with the ability to remember (a memory device). As knowledge is acquired, so is memory retained. The more the child knows, the more it can remember; the less it knows, the less it can remember; and if it knows nothing, it remembers nothing.

Form and function progress incrementally. As the body grows, so grows its craving for knowledge, and with knowledge, its ability to remember, to be aware of itself and its surroundings, leads it to a buoyant life.

Only a live body is capable of knowledge and remembering. Death, from the living perspectives, may also be defined as being devoid of knowledge and memory, in addition to the loss of the breath of life: "For the living know that they will die, but the dead *know nothing*, and they have no more reward, for the *memory of them is forgotten*."[38] Thus, the dead, from earthly perspectives, know nothing and can remember nothing. They have returned, to use the analogy of the earth, to the formless, empty and dark state.

---

[38] Ecclesiastes 9:5 (emphasis added)

By the same token, the state of death ought, by its nature, to be the most painless and obsidous[39] (non-responsive) state. The dead are formless, empty, and are in darkness. Death is the state of meaningless – an irresponsive, dreamless, nothingness and painless state. Death as a term, therefore, is more of a state than a place. It is the resultant event as knowledge fades and memory recedes. In essence, death may occur anytime the two conditions are met – the body becomes unable to inhale the air (breath of life) and both knowledge and memory are lost.

There may be situations in which the temporary state of death (stoppage of inhalation and exhalation of the breath of life or air) happens, and in which case the ability to know and remember still exists, the person may still be deemed to be alive. There may also be situations in which a person is able to breathe but can neither retain knowledge nor remember. This last state may conveniently be called incapacitation.

The first state may be more excruciating than the second. Where a person cannot breathe but

---

[39] Noun – obsidousness, a state of being painless, irresponsive, empty and formless.

is able to know and remember, the body will be in a state of flax and in this state people may experience the so-called out-of-body (oxygen-deficient) experiences. This state may be induced or may happen by natural means.

If suspended by magic or metaphysical crafts (witchcrafts), with the right treatment, the person may be returned to life but may be extremely weak and in a state of hallucination since the body has been deprived of the necessary breath of life or oxygen. Because such as may have this experience can still know and remember, they may be able to "float" up and observe themselves as they lie in a hopeful limbo. This experience may be encountered by people who are in coma (in some comatose situations, one may be able to retain some memory and even exercise some senses, e.g. the sense of hearing).

The second state, the state of incapacitation, may be said to be a state of indirect death, because the person can breathe but is unable to know or remember. They are alive as to the vital signs of life, but dead as to the real meaning of dying. Those are said to be brain-dead or who are on life-support machines, may be found in this category.

Neither incapacitation nor temporary death are true states of death. They are variants that may be brought about by varying circumstances (such as accidents), diseases or witchcraft. However, whether it began as incapacitation or temporary death, at some point, such a person will experience real death, an event that melts them into the nothing, from the human perspective.

Only those whose breath of life mechanisms have stopped, and who are unable to know and remember have truly gone past the ephemeral posture and have entered mortality, the state in which they can be said to be truly dead. In this state, neither medicinal nor incantational practices can make them return. They are gone and only by divine miracle, perhaps, are they able to be resurrected. At resurrection, they would have expiated the old frame but regained their old knowledge and memory and they could, after judgment, experience the new earth and its new essentials.

Breath of Life Exchange (BOLE)

"Then the LORD God formed a man from the dust of the ground and breathed into his nostrils the breath of life, and the man became a living being."[40]

There is a plain but subtly concealed truth that exists in our everyday respiration activities. Respiration may be viewed from three angles. In science, it is the inhalation of oxygen and the exhalation of carbondioxide. In our everyday living, it is called breathing – a process by which we sustain life. However, there is a third dimension, and it is called the Breath of Life Exchange or BOLE. At this dimension, breathing or respiration is a continuous exchange of the breath of life between it's source (God) and our bodies. In short, it is a continuous interlinkage between the natural and the divine. God keeps giving again and again of His spirit; and we keep giving back after use. Thus, life is maintained this way. Any delinkage means death. In other words, when God decides not to give it, we come up short and we have nothing to return to God, and we die. The process was initiated through the following act: "Then the LORD God formed

---

[40] Genesis 2:7

a man from the dust of the ground and breathed into his nostrils the breath of life, and the man became a living being."

BOLE is a process where we continue to receive God's spirit within us and to return after every use in a landlord-tenant-like repertoire. The giving by God is the blessing, and, to a lesser extend, the receiving, as the scripture says, "It is more blessed to give than to receive."[41] When it comes to BOLE, God is forever blessed.

BOLE implies three things. First, that we are alive at God's discretion: "…when you take away their breath, they die and return to the dust."[42] Humans are just a breath-withdrawal away from death. It is at God's determination, at His pleasure that they are alive. Second, that we are responsible for tending to the things of nostrils to ensure the breathing process is carried out. In other words, God's discretion must meet with our gratitude. Like a good tenant, we are responsible for taking good care of our breathing facilities. So long as God has not determined the withdrawal, we should tender and care for our lives. Doing things or

---

[41] Acts 20:35
[42] Psalm 104:29b

omitting to do things that promote life, is ingratitude. And third, we are not to do things that may cause our breathing stoppage. The termination of the tenancy lies to God, and not to the humans. Anything short of that may be called recklessness, suicide or homicide.

Thus, anything that kills a human being blocks the God-human breathing activity, and is, therefore, subject to the law of wrath.[43] One of the reasons why Jesus Christ came was to ensure that this God-human breathing activity becomes eternal. When God takes away life, it is because He has in mind another life, a more continuous and everlasting life: "The thief comes only to steal and kill and destroy; I came that they may have life, and have it abundantly."[44] Satan and murderers rob people of their lives, but God gives life. Satan kills people just when he knows they would go to Hell. Humans may kill another person just when that person is not ready to be saved. God, on the other hand, cannot terminate a person's life at the moment when that person is susceptible to eternal damnation: "The LORD said to Satan, 'Very well, then, everything he has is in your power, but on the

---

[43] Colossians 3:6; see also Romans 1:18
[44] John 10:10

man himself do not lay a finger.'"[45] In other words, God allowed Satan to oppress Job, but not to kill him. And that would be contrary to grace:

> For the grace of God has appeared, bringing salvation to everyone. It instructs us to renounce ungodliness and worldly passions, and to live sensible, upright, and godly lives in the present age, as we await the blessed hope and glorious appearance of our great God and Savior Jesus Christ.[46]

Grace saves, and sustains life till resurrection. God neither does evil nor perverts justice: "It is unthinkable that God would do wrong, that the Almighty would pervert justice."[47] And it is God who is so concerned about people dying in sin that He has even solicited for prayer to increase the labor force: "Then He said to His disciples, 'The harvest is plentiful, but the workers are few. Ask the Lord of the harvest, therefore, to send out workers into His

---

[45] Job 1:12
[46] Titus 2:11-13
[47] Job 34:12

harvest.""[48] Satan's goal is to harvest dead souls into Hell; God's is to save souls for eternity.

So, what does BOLE remind us? It shows us that the human race (and all living things for that matter) exhibits God's generosity towards life through their breathing activities. Every pulse of the heart and every respiratory functionality, clearly show that God is gracious. People should be grateful to God and honor Him for the gift of breathing that they utilize every time they respire. When God stops it, they expire.

It is estimated that, "Your heart beats about 100,000 times in one day and about 35 million times in a year. During an average lifetime, the human heart will beat more than 2.5 billion times."[49] And a person may take an amazing over 670,000,000 breaths in their average 80 year lifetime: "On average, a person at rest takes about 16 breaths per minute. This means we breathe about 960 breaths an hour, 23,040 breaths a day, 8,409,600 a year. Unless we get a

---

[48] Matthew 9:37-38
[49] https://www.pbs.org/wgbh/nova/heart/heartfacts.html#:~: text=Your%20heart%20beats%20about%20100%2C000,ball%20a%20good%2C%20hard%20squeeze. Accessed on August 7th, 2022.

lot of exercise. The person who lives to 80 will take about 672,768,000 breaths in a lifetime."[50] With each of the about 2.5 billion heartbeats, and the over 670 million breaths in an average lifetime, our generous response should be to live for the good of all humanity and its planet, and for the glory of God. That would be the best way of the wise use of BOLE.

Time

Death and time are inversely related, where one is, the other stops. Life begins time; death ends it. Time only impacts the mortals, not the divine and the immortals. It establishes purpose and governs activities. Death can also be defined as the end of time; nothing happens in death, time stands still. Every heartbeat corresponds to the rhythm of life. The first thing that stops when a person dies, is the beating of the heart.

Without time, age is suspended – therefore, the old and the young are only so because of time. God cannot age because He does not live

---

[50] http://sites.dartmouth.edu/estimation/files/2016/11/breathing.docx#:~:text=Solution%3A%20On%20average%2C%20a%20person,672%2C768%2C000%20breaths%20in%20a%20lifetime. Accessed on August 7th, 2022.

within time. Humans and animals age because they live within time. Therefore, with God, those who died thousands of years ago are as if they just went to sleep yesterday. When the resurrection happens, God will be familiar with everyone who ever lived.

During death, time is suspended, which means that when the dead are finally resurrected, they would have missed nothing since they died. Their reality will be the same as those who died a second before the resurrection. Thus, when Judgment Day comes, it will vindicate some and condemn others – since all will be judged only according to what they did when they were alive.

Death is subconscious rest, unlike the conscious rest people experience when they exist in time. Consciousness is only effective with time. Without time, consciousness is inactive and without effect. During the state of unconsciousness, one is temporarily out of time, but they still remain alive as long as one of the three elements of life are present: Breath, knowledge or memory.

If time was eliminated, people would either be alive forever or would be dead forever.

Therefore, they would not age. They would exist permanently, forever. The reason is because time would be no more.

Time is responsible for change of states, say, of matter, from liquid to solid to gas. It is responsible for changes of day to night to day. It is responsible for the changes of ages from young to old. It is responsible for the changes of moods, character and predispositions. It is responsible for the changes in seasons. It affects everything that changes.

Without time, everything remains in the same state they find themselves – good remains good and bad remains bad. Thus, after the resurrection, the bad may not be made good and the good may not be made bad. The only time to change is before one dies.

All religions – those who believe in reincarnation and those who believe in resurrection – believe that there is an after-life. The assumption is that when a person dies, they go to another life. The only seeming variance is the question of time. Some believe that immediately one dies, they instantly inherit Paradise or Hell. Others believe that there is a waiting period; that death happens in stages. Both may be right and wrong at the same time.

In the first place, resurrection (for those who believe in it) will not happen sporadically; it will take place at the same time for everyone. This fact, therefore, eliminates varying periods of resurrections. Those who died thousands of years ago will be resurrected at the same time as those who would have died yesterday if resurrection were to happen today.

In the case of reincarnation, there is an assumption of time – that one is eventually reborn into another form, animal or plant. In this new form, the realities of the first form (good or bad) are muted. The new form is exactly that, new. It neither remembers nor experiences its old form.

Therefore, even to those who believe in reincarnation, death ends the reality of the first form. If reincarnation is efficacious, it means that each time a person reincarnates, they return to time, and therefore, it creates a vicious cycle of re-experiences, and thence, still in the process of awaiting the final exist in which time is no more and the past deeds are judged. Death stops time.

In the second place, since death ends time, whether through resurrection or reincarnation, the final formation will be the immediate return of memory of the previous life. For resurrection, this means the previous life in which the subject existed. For reincarnation, however, it would be the previous lives in which the subject had existed. It, therefore, does not make one better than the other or more exculpatory than the other.

Whether they resurrect or reincarnate, the final judgment will deal with the previous life or lives, respectively. What is truthful is that when time is suspended at death, everyone will rise at the same time, as if it was just yesterday when they died.

The teaching of Islam is cogent on this point: "Muslims believe that on a day decided by Allah, and known only to Allah, life on earth will come to an end and Allah will destroy everything. On this day all the people who have ever lived will be raised from the dead and will face judgement by Allah. Muslims believe that they *will remain in their graves until this day*. This day is called by several names: the Day of Resurrection (Yawm al-Qiyamah); the Day of

Judgment (Yawm al-Din); the Last Hour (as-sa'a)."[51]

And the Quran also says, "Every soul shall taste death, and only on the Day of Judgment will you be paid your full recompense."[52]

The Islamic belief on death corresponds, partly, to the Christian view. The Bible says, "And just as each person is destined to die once and after that comes judgment."[53]

Buddhists believe in reincarnation. Their central thesis is that there is a cycle of life – life, death and rebirth. They believe that a person's spirit remains close by and seeks out a new body and new life. Buddhists, thus, see life and death as a continuum. The conception of spirit is the same as consciousness. The first thing that perishes at death is knowledge and last, it is memory (or consciousness).

---

[51] BBC, "Afterlife (akhirah),"
https://www.bbc.co.uk/bitesize/guides/ztyvxfr/revision/2#:~:text=Muslims%20believe%20that%20on%20a,will%20face%20judgement%20by%20Allah accessed on July 16th, 2022 (Emphasis added).
[52] Quran 3:185
[53] Hebrews 9:27 (New Living Translation Bible)

From the point of view of dying, it does not matter that one believes in reincarnation, *vis*, that the spirit continues after death and may be reborn. What is assumed in Buddhistic expostulation is that when death happens, judgment follows – whether that judgment be actionable here on earth through reincarnation or through resurrection. Both resurrection and reincarnation can only be possible after time is first suspended through the experience of death.

The idea of time and dying has been a bone of contention even among the most vested of religious scholars, especially in Christianity. Just at what point does a person die and then reap the benefits of a life they lived? Is it instantaneously or it takes place at some time in the far future?

The aforementioned Bible scripture[54] seems to suggest that it is instantaneously. And the confusion is not eased when one reads the following Bible scripture: "One day the beggar died and was carried by the angels to Abraham's side. And the rich man also died and was buried. In Hades, where he was in

---

[54] See Hebrews 9:27, *supra*.

torment, he looked up and saw Abraham from afar, with Lazarus by his side."[55]

These verses precede a narrative about a poor man called Lazarus who ate the crumbs that fell from the rich man's table. The assumption in this passage of the Bible is that the rich man lived an unrighteous life and Lazarus lived a morally upright life. The passage, though, does not assume that all poor people are righteous and neither does it presuppose that all rich people will go to Hell.

What brings Hebrews 9:27 and Luke 16:22-23 into contention is their seeming assumptions that immediately one dies, they immediately experience judgment – for good or for bad. That assumption derogates from the ambit of time and death, and postulates that once time ends (death) immediately judgment begins.

And if that assumption holds, it means that people are judged immediately they die. It will then eliminate the doctrine of resurrection and reincarnation completely from religious discourse. That belief will not only be faulty, but it goes against the grains of biblical or quranical motifs.

---
[55] Luke 16:22-23

Apostle Paul argues vehemently against that heresy: "If there is no resurrection of the dead, then not even Christ has been raised. And if Christ has not been raised, our preaching is worthless, and so is your faith. In that case, we are also exposed as false witnesses about God. For we have testified about God that He raised Christ from the dead, but He did not raise Him if in fact the dead are not raised. And if Christ has not been raised, your faith is futile; you are still in your sins."[56]

The doctrine of resurrection, for Christians, is the lynchpin of the august faith and on it hinges all the structure and functionality of its belief system.

Therefore, there will be a resurrection for Christians and Muslims, and for Buddhists and Hindus, there might be reincarnation. In both cases, time is relevant to the core of their belief systems. While for both Muslims and Buddhists the conception of time vis-à-vis death is assumed, and even presumed, in Christianity, the verses aforecited, seem to presume immediacy.

---

[56] 1 Corinthians 15:13-17

However, critical review and taking the core of Christianity as a whole, the Bible is very explicit and clear on the interaction of life, time and death. In both Hebrews 9 and Luke 16, the idea of time is presumed. In Luke, we read, "One day the beggar died and was carried by the angels to Abraham's side. And the rich man also died and was buried." Both of them died. We read that Lazarus was carried by angels to the bosom of Abraham, but the rich man was only buried and we don't hear anything until the rich man rediscovered the soul of Lazarus, albeit in two different places separated by a chasm.

The confusion often comes when Luke alludes to the presence of angels and the immediate conception is that immediately Lazarus dies, he is transported to Heaven. The immediate interpretation of this scripture may be that, at some point after the resurrection, Lazarus was taken into the presence of Abraham by angels. Not before the resurrection. And the extended conception, going with the ambit of Hebrews 9 is that, this entire transportation occurred after judgment, for "It is appointed for man to die once, and after that, judgment." In this regard, Luke 16 is more of an allegorical than of a factual account. But this would be problematic as it will be expounded further later.

The Bible, clearly, implies the suspension of time in death, and where time is involved, the Bible makes it explicit. For example, in Genesis 1 and 2, Moses discusses the creation of the earth. Moses clearly specifies where time is linear, that the creation of the earth happened in seven days.

He, then lays out the transition: Day 1, light; Day 2, atmosphere or the firmament; Day 3, dry ground and plants; Day 4, the sun, the moon and the stars; Day 5, the birds and all sea creatures; Day 6, the land animals and humans; and Day 7, God rested in a Sabbath. It is important to clarify that the light that God created on Day 1 is not the sun; the sun was only created on Day 4. Thus, too many times, people may overlook details in order to vie for the mundane. In other words, the sun is only one source of light.

It is also important to note, as far as time is concerned, that there is, definitely, a big gap between the creation of the heavens and the earth. This account reveals that Moses meant literal days and not figurative millennia. And an abridge to this explanation is found in what God did on the seventh day; He rested. Saturday is a Sabbath, a day of rest. If Saturday was only a metaphorical day, adherents of Judaism and the Seventh Day Adventists would have been in a permanent state of rest for a millennium. The account of Genesis 1 and 2 does not reveal how God made Heaven. The "heavens" of Genesis 1 and 2 clearly refer to earth's atmosphere, sometimes called the expanse or space.

Moses writes, "In the beginning God created the heavens and the earth."[57] Moses does not give an account of how Heaven or Hell were created. It can be inferred from Genesis 1 and 2 that God was in Heaven when He created the "heavens and the earth." So, what does it then mean when Moses indicates that his account is traced from "in the beginning"?

Does this mean that it was the beginning of time? Absolutely. That is the only plausible conclusion.

The correct rendition of Genesis 1:1 should read as: "When time began (or in the beginning of time) God created the heavens and the

---

[57] Genesis 1:1

earth." For it is only what exists in the earth and around the earth that exists within time; spiritual beings may theophanize, occasionally, to penetrate time spaces. This capacity they have, but humans do not have it until they die or are raptured. Humans, though, have the capacity to reach anywhere on earth and its space. God, angels, the devil and his demons do not live within time. Humans and animals must be alive to live within time. Death to them means the end of time.

After the resurrection and judgment, humans will live, like God and angels, out of time. They will live forever: "For they cannot die anymore, because they are equal to angels and are sons of God, being sons of the resurrection."[58] Death may happen twice, but the final resurrection only once. Once a person dies, that person only awaits the resurrection when they will rise to be rewarded or condemned.

The condemnation of those who have resurrected is casually called the "Second Death" in the Bible: "[A]s for the cowardly, the faithless, the polluted, the murderers, the fornicators, the sorcerers, the idolaters, and all liars, their place will be in the lake that burns

---

[58] Luke 20:36

with fire and sulfur, which is the second death."[59]

The first death takes the souls of the righteous and the unrighteous alike. However, it takes them to different places. The second death has no rest - "Where their worm does not die and their fire is not quenched."[60] The meaning of unquenchable fire is clear. However, the meaning of the worm that never dies is unclear.

What is clear is that the second death will trigger serious eternal consequences for those who are affected by it. Perhaps the following commentary may lend some insight: "'Worm' is from the Greek root word *scolex* and refers to a maggot that eats dead flesh. The fact that it does not die suggests a varying meaning, although scholars are not sure what. Both this verse and Isaiah 66:24 say, 'their worm,' meaning [that] it may be something the

---

[59] Revelation 21:8; see also Revelation 20:14; Revelation 2:11; Revelation 20:6; and Jude 1:12, which appears to refer to it as "doubly dead," "These are the men who are hidden reefs in your love feasts when they feast with you without fear, caring for themselves; clouds without water, carried along by winds; autumn trees without fruit, *doubly dead*, uprooted" (emphasis added).
[60] Mark 9:44; see also Mark 9:48

unbeliever brought with them, *perhaps their shame and regret.*"[61]

In Judaism, the second death seems to be identical with judgment, following the resurrection.[62] Indeed, the second death is not death in the nominal sense of the first death because the second death, is not a state; it is a place.

The good news is that, in the Christian Bible, God has provided a way of salvation for all people through grace: "For the grace of God that brings salvation has appeared to *all men.*"[63] This is, perhaps, one of the greatest revelations in the Christian Bible. In short, in Christianity, God has provided every human being with a chance to be saved. How He does this, is the Supreme Being's will and secret. The issue, according to this verse, is not the opportunity, it is the willingness of people to believe and repent when such a chance comes, and it will come, for everyone. That's why it is called grace.

---

[61] "What does Mark 9:48 mean?" < https://www.bibleref.com/Mark/9/Mark-9-48.html> accessed on July 17th, 2022 (emphasis added).
[62] Harry Sysling (1996), "Teḥiyyat ha-metim: the resurrection of the dead in the Palestinian," *Targums,* p. 222
[63] Titus 2:11 (emphasis added)

Islam has a different take on this. According to Islam, only believers in God can receive salvation. Disbelievers in God do not receive salvation. In Islam, implicitly, it is believed that believers in God who are non-Muslims (such as Christians, Buddhists, and etc.) can be saved. However, this is left to God's discretion (God's will) to save or not to save.

Thus, for Islam, the authority for salvation is both divine ("the will of Allah") and legalistic, contained within the law, the Shariah Law. And the method of salvation is strictly formulaic, a slogan called *shahada*, the Muslim profession of faith that, "There is no god but Allah, and Muhammad is the messenger of Allah." Accordingly, in Islam, a good life pleasing to Allah can earn one salvation.

In theory, all the major religions of the world offer their adherents a cogent way of salvation in or after death. In practice, however, the doctrine of grace espoused by Christianity is more concrete. And in Chapter 2, the elements of the Triphemeral Dimensions of the Patch (TDP) are clearly explained. These are the subconscious, the subcortical, and the subphemeral patches. Through these, humans are capable of discerning death, and determining exactly how they may want to die.

Stages of Death

According to the Vedas, a collection of revered Hindu texts, all beings are souls and thus spiritual in nature. Although the body is temporary and eventually dies, the soul is eternal.[64] Hindus believe that each soul is on a journey of spiritual development facilitated in part by *Karma*. That theory seems to support the basis that death happens in stages. Thus, "After a loved one dies, the goal of the family is to help the departing soul transition to the next life. It's therefore encouraged to have the funeral as soon as possible — ideally within 24 hours — so that a soul can begin the journey to its next destination."[65]

The Hindus cremate their dead as a way of freeing them to the next phase. The soul is said to be encased by both a physical and subtle (non-physical) body. After the physical body dies, the subtle body continues to function,

---

[64] Syama Allard, "5 things to know about Hindus and death," September 3rd, 2020, <
https://www.hinduamerican.org/blog/5-things-to-know-about-hindus-and-death> accessed on July 31st, 2022
[65] Ibid.

through which the soul moves on to its next destination. But because so many attachments form throughout life, it can be difficult for a soul to transition, causing it to linger.[66] All beings are eternal and spiritual, whereas the physical body is temporary. Thus, Hindus cremate the body as a way of freeing the soul from this life so that it can move on to the next.[67]

The Quran, the Islamic holy book, says: "Nor can a soul die except by Allah's leave. The term being fixed as by writing."[68] However, in Islam, the concept of stages of death is widely believed in. In fact, Muslims believe that the soul of a person passes through fourteen (14) stages. These are:[69] Barzakh; Blowing of the Trumpet; Apocalypse or Qiyama; Resurrection after death; Gathering Place; Receiving the Book of Deeds; Reckoning; Scale or Mizan; River and Pool of Kawthar; Sirat; Intercession; Purgatory; Hell; and Paradise.

Barzakh is like a waiting room. Blowing of the Trumpet is done by the angel Hazrat Israfel. By

---

[66] Ibid.
[67] Ibid.
[68] Quran 3:145
[69] https://zamzam.com/blog/life-after-death-in-islam/ (accessed on July 31st, 2022)

blowing the trumpet twice, Hazrat takes the dead to the gathering place. In the Qiyama, the dead rise and walk towards the gathering place. At this stage, the Quran says, "O mankind! fear your Lord! For the convulsion of the Hour (of Judgment) will be a thing terrible! The Day ye shall see it, every mother giving suck shall forget her suckling-babe, and every pregnant female shall drop her load (unformed): thou shalt see mankind as in a drunken riot, yet not drunk: but dreadful will be the Wrath of Allah."[70]

Then the resurrection after death will happen. Here, the dead are lifted from their graves and are brought before Allah to be judged for their deeds. From here, there is the Gathering Place – where they wait to receive the Book of Deeds. Receiving the Book of Deeds is the stage where the souls are gathered together to receive the Book of Deeds, which has the records of their good and bad deeds. From here, comes the Reckoning. This is where the souls are judged equally.

The Quran says here, thus, "That Day will every soul be requited for what it earned; no injustice will there be that Day, for Allah is

---

[70] Al-Hajj, 1-2

swift in taking account."[71] After the Reckoning is the Mizan. Here, souls are weighed in a scale. "If a person's good deeds have more weight than the bad ones, then they get salvation, and if good deeds are lighter than bad deeds, they suffer punishment.

This is akin to the weighing of evidence in common-law judicial procedures. When the probative value of the evidence outweighs its prejudicial effect, the material may be tendered as evidence and, eventually, used in reaching a decision. This view also supports the standard of proof on the balance of probabilities. Thus, there is discretion on the part of Allah to be lenient where he can.

It is also said that believers who go to Hell can also be sent to Paradise after completing their punishment.[72] Then souls enter into the River and Pool of Kawthar – where Prophet Hazrat Muhammad has the pre-eminence. However, whoever reaches the pool first will be made prophet. From there comes Sirat, a bridge across Hell. Every soul is expected to cross it. From the bridge comes Intercession – where those who have committed certain sins ask the

---

[71] al-Mumin, 17
[72] https://zamzam.com/blog/life-after-death-in-islam/, *supra*.

scholars and prophets to beg Allah (God) for forgiveness, and those who do not have any sin ask to be raised to a higher level.[73] Intercession leads to Purgatory, which is a chasm that separates Hell and Paradise. Hell (or Jahannam) is the next stage, and here souls with worst deeds enter, are tortured and punished for their sins. The last stage is Paradise, where only those with good deeds enter to live in eternal comfort. And the Quran is clear-cut on this: "Of the good that they do nothing will be rejected of them; for Allah knoweth well those that do right. Those who reject faith – neither their possessions nor their (numerous) progeny will avail them aught against Allah; they will be companions of the fire, dwelling therein forever."[74]

In Christianity, the idea of stages is rarely directly contemplated. There are some inferential implications here and there. For example, the soul is said to depart when a person dies. Departing has a connotation of going on a trip: "And as her soul was departing (for she was dying), she called his name Ben-oni; but his father called him Benjamin."[75]

---

[73] Ibid.
[74] Quran 3:115- 1:116
[75] Genesis 35:18

The idea of "entering" at some gate or door is very prominent in the Bible. For example, Jesus tells a Jewish Pharisee that he could not enter the Kingdom of God unless he was born-again: "Jesus replied, 'Truly, truly, I tell you, no one can see the kingdom of God unless he is born again.'"[76] Jesus also claimed to be the door: "I am the door: by me if any man enter in, he shall be saved, and shall go in and out, and find pasture."[77] And to Christians, Paradise may be in the form of a city where all with sin cannot enter: "Blessed are those who wash their robes, so that they may have the right to the *tree of life* and may enter the city by its gates. But *outside* are the dogs, the sorcerers, the sexually immoral, the murderers, the idolaters, and everyone who loves and practices falsehood."[78]

The Bible places Paradise somewhere on earth, which might have first existed in the form of a Garden of Eden. In this garden, there was neither tedious work nor death. However, after humanity (Adam and Eve) sinned, God removed them from the garden and proscribed

---

[76] John 3:3
[77] John 10:9
[78] Revelation 22:15 (emphasis added)

them from reaching the Tree of Life therein: "Therefore, the LORD God banished him from the Garden of Eden to work the ground from which he had been taken. So, He drove out the man and stationed cherubim on the east side of the Garden of Eden, along with a whirling sword of flame to guard the way to the tree of life."[79] Interestingly, as presaged by John Milton in his concept of a *Paradise Lost*, indeed, Paradise was lost by an act of sin, but only to be regained by an act of grace:

> Then he showed me a river of the water of life, clear as crystal, coming from the throne of God and of the Lamb, in the middle of its street. On either side of the river was the *tree of life*, bearing twelve kinds of fruit, yielding its fruit every month; and the leaves of the tree were for the healing of the nations. There will no longer be any curse; and the throne of God and of the Lamb will be in it, and His bond-servants will serve Him.[80]

The combination of Genesis 3 and Revelation 21 and 22 show that, first, God did not destroy the Garden of Eden; it exists somewhere in

---

[79] Genesis 3:23-24
[80] Revelation 22:1-3, emphasis added)

some form. Second, that the Tree of Life still stands there under guard. Third, that there is no mention of the Tree of Knowledge of Good and Evil in the new Paradise – because we all know that it was the one that led to the experience of death and suffering on earth through man's disobedience. And fourth, that the Tree of Life resurfaces in the New Jerusalem, which we may naively call Paradise. This, too, is sufficient to conclude that Paradise may not be Heaven, because this city comes out of Heaven: "I saw the Holy City, the New Jerusalem, *coming down out of heaven from God*, prepared as a bride beautifully dressed for her husband."[81]

The consolation is that, the city does not come to an old, sinful earth; it, rather, comes to a renewed earth: "Then I saw '*a new heaven and a new earth*,' for the first heaven and the first earth had *passed away*, and there was no longer any sea."[82] The New International Version (NIV) rendition of Revelation 21:1 may be the exact translation because it puts "a new heaven and a new earth" in quotation marks. The allusion to "passed away [died]" is further refined by the following verse: "For behold, I will create

---

[81] Revelation 21:2 (emphasis added)
[82] Revelation 21:1 (emphasis added)

new heavens and a new earth. The former things will *not be remembered, nor will they come to mind.*"[83] In the new order, memory, relative to the evils of the old order, will disappear. This will be a miraculous transformation that will come with the resurrected or raptured bodies which would have undergone the judgment for rewards. This verse of scripture, too, brings clarity to Revelation 21:1, the "heaven" of this verse in Revelation, in fact, represents the "heavens" of Isaiah 65. And this is in order, because what will be refined or refreshed or remodelled, is not Heaven, the Throne of God; it is the expanse or space. The earth has been in a fallen state (state of corruption) ever sin entered into the world and Satan was thrown to the earth:

> "They have conquered him by the blood of the Lamb and by the word of their testimony. And they did not love their lives so as to shy away from death. Therefore, rejoice, O *heavens*, and you who dwell in them! But woe to the earth and the sea; with great fury the devil has come down to you, knowing he has only a short time." And when the dragon saw that he

---

[83] Isaiah 65:17 (emphasis added)

> had been thrown to the earth, he pursued the woman who had given birth to the male child.[84]

Two facts are clear, one is unclear in these verses of scripture. First, in terms of clarity, Satan was chased away from Heaven. And second, he is currently on earth with great fury. But what is unclear is the reference to "heavens," which, in this context may easily refer to Heaven. It may not include the earth's atmosphere because Satan would easily have access to that part of the universe just as he has to earth. Moreover, the entire creation (the heavens and the earth) has been in agony: "For the creation was subjected to *futility*, not by its own will, but because of the One who subjected it, in hope that the creation itself will be set free from its *bondage to decay* and brought into the glorious freedom of the children of God."[85]

In other words, creation has been corrupted, the heavens and earth, included. Indeed, Satan's rule is also known as "ruler of the kingdom of the air."[86] "Air" in this context may

---

[84] Revelation 12:11-13 (emphasis added)
[85] Romans 8:20-21 (emphasis added)
[86] Ephesians 2:2

mean the heavens, the atmosphere or space. The use of "heavens" in Revelation 12:11-13 is akin to "heavenlies," a realm of grace, in which according to the Pauline Theology, the exemplification of redeemer-saints existence happens in an intricate spiritual state:

> Praise be to the God and Father of our Lord Jesus Christ, who has blessed us in the *heavenly realms* with every spiritual blessing in Christ.…[He] made us alive with Christ even when we were dead in our trespasses. It is by *grace* you have been saved! And God raised us up with Christ and seated us with Him in the *heavenly realms* in Christ Jesus, in order that in the coming ages He might display the surpassing riches of His grace, demonstrated by His kindness to us in Christ Jesus.[87]

The heavenly realm or the heavenlies is neither the earth's atmosphere nor Heaven. It is a special place of grace where believers in Christ, spiritually, enjoy their interaction with Christ Jesus. It also seems to be a place where sin and Satan cannot touch them. It happens only to those who are "in Christ," who have,

---

[87] Ephesians 1:3; 2:5-7

symbolically, died and have been raised, by faith, with Christ. In this grace-founded, faith-based place, believers have access, while here on earth and alive, to all good things (blessings) that are theirs in Christ Jesus.

To tie up, the word "heavens" needs context for interpretation purposes. Generally, God created everything, including the "heavens" (as opposed to the earth), and the earth and the seas. The heavens, though, seem to be ordered in degrees of glory, with God's throne being in what is called "the heaven of heaven"[88] or the "third heaven,"[89] or the "highest heaven." This is captured by Moses, thus, "To the LORD your God belong the heavens, even the *highest heavens*, the earth and everything in it."[90] It is speculative that the first and second heavens may correspond to the heavens (atmosphere or expanse) and what the Bible refers to as "kingdom of the air." The location of the *heavenlies* is unclear, and it is reasonable to conclude that it is a spiritual abode and may even be around or in the third heaven.

---

[88] Psalm 115:16 (Douay-Rheims Bible)

[89] 2 Corinthians 12:2

[90] Deuteronomy 10:14 (emphasis added)

In Christianity, there is an assumption that a person who dies may be in some sort of transition, probably through these heavens. The story of raising Lazarus from the dead is key here: "And when he thus had spoken, he cried with a loud voice, Lazarus, *come forth*. And he that was dead *came forth*, bound hand and foot with graveclothes: and his face was bound about with a napkin. Jesus saith unto them, Loose him, and let him go."[91] Some might construe the phrase "come forth" as if Lazars was on a journey from which he would be returning.

And the account of another Lazarus (a poor beggar) and a rich man also seems to suggest that there are some sort of a transitory stage in death:

> And it came to pass, that the beggar died, and was *carried* by the angels into Abraham's bosom: the rich man also died, and was buried; And in Hell he lift up his eyes, being in torments, and seeth Abraham afar off, and Lazarus in his bosom. And he cried and said, Father Abraham, have mercy on me, and send Lazarus, that he may

---

[91] John 11:43-44 (emphasis added)

> dip the tip of his finger in water, and cool my tongue; for I am tormented in this flame. But Abraham said, Son, *remember* that thou in thy lifetime receivedst thy good things, and likewise Lazarus evil things: but now he is comforted, and thou art tormented. And beside all this, *between us and you there is a great gulf fixed: so that they which would pass from hence to you cannot; neither can they pass to us, that would come from thence.*[92]

Here, angels "carried" Lazarus, and the Abrahams figure informs the rich man that there is a "gulf fixed...so that they which would pass from hence to you cannot; neither can they pass to us, that would come from thence." In this account, the burying of Lazarus and the rich man does not end their journey into death. This truth is acknowledged by all key religions. The dead, at some point, embark on some form of a journey towards absolution. Jesus, in the story of Lazarus and the rich man is suggesting that the dead can remember and feel:

> He answered, 'Then I beg you, father, send Lazarus to my family,

---

[92] Luke 16:22-26 (emphasis added)

> *for I have five brothers.* Let him warn them, so that they will not also come to this place of torment.' "Abraham replied, 'They have Moses and the Prophets; let them listen to them.' "'No, Father Abraham,' he said, 'but if someone from the dead goes to them, they will repent.' "He said to him, 'If they do not listen to Moses and the Prophets, they will not be convinced even if someone rises from the dead.'"[93]

This account seems literally and not parabolical. It seems like a real story rather than a parable or allegory. Jesus spoke of Moses and the Prophets. The rich dead man spoke of having relatives still alive on earth. This dead man remembered. He also felt.

The question is not whether there is a transition into the after-life; the question is at what point? Do they do so after the resurrection or before? According to the Christian teachings, this could be interpreted either way.

---

[93] Luke 16: 27-31, *supra.*

In the other passage of the raising of Lazarus, Jesus confirms that death is a sleep, albeit a very long and perpetual sleep: "These things said he: and after that he saith unto them, Our friend Lazarus *sweepeth*; but I go, that I may *awake him out of sleep*. Then said his disciples, Lord, if he sleep, he shall do well. Howbeit Jesus spake of his *death*: but they thought that *he had spoken of taking of rest in sleep*. Then said Jesus unto them plainly, Lazarus is *dead*."[94]

It is also true that this is not a normal kind of sleep. In sleep, people breathe, dream, and even remember. In death, however, people cease all respiratory activities. In fact, they are buried and they decay. In the case of Lazarus, the cousin of Jesus, he had been dead for four days and he was decaying. He had been clinically dead. It is also true from Scripture that Lazarus was not in Heaven, because, as Jesus said, no-one has ever been to Heaven except Jesus Himself: "If I have told you about earthly things and you do not believe, how will you believe if I tell you about heavenly things? *No one has ascended into heaven except the One who descended from heaven*— the Son of Man."[95]

---

[94] John 11:11-14 (emphasis added)
[95] John 3:13 (emphasis added)

The argument could be had that raising people from the dead is only possible if they have been dead for a short period of time. However, the incident at the resurrection of Jesus Christ proves otherwise: "The tombs broke open, and the bodies of many saints who had fallen asleep were raised. After Jesus' resurrection, when they had come out of the tombs, they entered the holy city and appeared to many people."[96] These people, it is assumed, had been dead for a long time. And some rose up and joined life in the city. Even here, we see that they rose with their bodies intact, and the assumption is that their dead bodies were revived.

The event is akin to Elijah's in the Old Testament:

> After this the son of the woman, the mistress of the house became ill. And his illness was so severe that *there was no breath left in him* And she said to Elijah, "What have you against me, O man of God? You have come to me to bring my sin and remembrance and to cause the death of my son!" And he stretched himself upon the child three times, and cried unto the Lord, and said,

---

[96] Matthew 27:52-53

> "O Lord my God, I pray thee, let this child's *soul come into him again.*" And the Lord heard the voice of Elijah; and *the soul of the child came into him again, and he revived.*[97]

Two facts come out from the preceding scriptures. First, that death is the separation of the soul from the body. The soul is eternal; but the body can decay. In fact, the body begins to decay immediately its soul leaves it. And second, that when the soul returns into its body, the body can begin to live, to revive. This was the case with Lazarus, the young man, the young son and those who rose again at Jesus' resurrection.

The resurrection that comes from God automatically brings healing to the revived body: "Then He walked over and touched the coffin, while the pallbearers stood still. Jesus said to the dead man, 'Young man, I say to thee, arise!' And he who was dead, sat up and began to talk, and Jesus gave him back to his mother."[98]

Similarly, a body without the soul is cold. Most people testify to dying when their bodies begin

---

[97] 1 Kings 17:17-22 (emphasis added)
[98] Luke 7:14

to lose heat. A live body has warmth because it has its soul in it:

> When Elisha came into the house, he saw the child lying dead on his bed. So he went in and shut the door behind the two of them and prayed to the Lord. Then he went up and lay on the child, putting his mouth on his mouth, his eyes on his eyes, and his hands on his hands. And as he stretched himself upon him, the flesh of *the child became warm*. Then he got up again and walked once back and forth in the house, and went up and stretched himself upon him. The child sneezed seven times, and the child opened his eyes.[99]

There is an event in the New Testament in which Eutychus dozes off during Paul's lengthy sermon and dies. Paul brings Eutychus back to life:

> On the first day of the week we came together to break bread. Paul spoke to the people and, because he intended to leave the next day, kept on talking until midnight. There were many lamps in the

---

[99] 2 Kings 4: 32-35 (emphasis added)

> upstairs room where we were meeting. Seated in a window was a young man named Eutychus, who was sinking into a deep sleep as Paul talked on and on. When he was sound asleep, he fell to the ground from the third story and was picked up dead. Paul went down, threw himself on the young man and put his arms around him. "Don't be alarmed," he said. "He's alive!" Then he went upstairs again and broke bread and ate. After talking until daylight, he left. The people took the young man home alive and were greatly comforted.[100]

However, a notable observation is that all those who died and were raised, there was a compelling reason for raising them up. The most compelling reason was pity or compassion or the combination of the two.

This was the case with Elijah, Elisha, Jesus or Paul. And each of those who rose from the dead, there is no doubt, they died again. Their type of resurrection may conveniently be termed "Partial Resurrection" because they died again and are waiting for the final resurrection when they will face judgment. A

---

[100] Acts 20:7-12

case can also be made that those who have died so far, have not undergone judgment.

This is the only plausible explanation. If they had been judged, they would have been in their permanent abode of either Heaven or Hell. Inference can be drawn that the souls of those who died in faith do rest, like in a deep sleep, and those who did not believe may be in a place like in the one the rich man in Luke 16 found himself.

In other words, this type of rising (partial resurrection) is not categorized as the resurrection that some will undergo before Judgment Day. The final resurrection is one of the central tenets of the Christian faith and doctrine. It is the doctrine (creed) of rising back to life after death. Christians believe that Jesus Christ died and came back to life again by the power of the Holy Spirit.

They also believe that since Jesus rose again from the dead, they will also be raised from the dead at the end of the age. Apostle Paul argues that, if the resurrection doesn't exist, Christianity doesn't exist, either: "And if Christ has not been raised, our preaching is useless and so is your faith." The implication is that, there is a final resurrection.

Some Christians will not die. However, they will be transformed into bodies such as Jesus had after He rose again from the dead on the third day. Christians who will not die may be raptured. Christian believers believe that when Jesus comes again for the second time, He will first "rapture," or take out of the earth in bodily form, all those who had died in faith and those who will be alive.

Apostle Paul declares it this way: "For the Lord Himself will descend from heaven with a loud command, with the voice of an archangel, and with the trumpet of God, and the dead in Christ will be the first to rise. After that, we who are alive and remain will be caught up together with them in the clouds to meet the Lord in the air. And so we will always be with the Lord."[101]

The Jesus-kind of post-resurrection bodies are special. They can pass through walls or doors: "That Sunday evening the disciples were meeting behind locked doors because they were afraid of the Jewish leaders. Suddenly,

---

[101] 1 Thessalonians 4:16-17

Jesus was standing there among them! 'Peace be with you,' he said."[102]

And they can even penetrate into Heaven: "After He had said this, they watched as He was taken up, and a cloud hid Him from their sight… 'Men of Galilee,' they said, 'why do you stand here looking into the sky? This same Jesus, who has been taken from you into heaven, will come back in the same way you have seen Him go into heaven.'"[103] These special bodies cannot be harmed by death:

> In a moment, in the twinkling of an eye, at the last trumpet. For the trumpet will sound, and the dead will be raised imperishable, and we shall be changed. For this perishable body must put on the imperishable, and this mortal body must put on immortality. When the perishable puts on the imperishable, and the mortal puts on immortality, then shall come to pass the saying that is written: "Death is swallowed up in victory."[104]

---

[102] John 20:19 (New Living Translation (NLT))
[103] Acts 1:9 and 11; see also Mark 16:19
[104] 1 Corinthians 15:52-54; see also 1 John 3:2

Therefore, not everyone will taste death: "Truly I tell you, some who are standing here will not taste death before they see the Son of Man coming in His kingdom."[105] As to whether Jesus meant those who were listening to Him at that time, is unclear. What is clear, however, is the inference to Rapture, which the Apostle Paul had occasion to clarify in the New Testament.[106]

The ambit of Hebrews 9 must be taken in context. "Just as man is appointed to die once, and after that to face judgment, so also Christ was offered once to bear the sins of many; and He will appear a second time, not to bear sin, but to bring salvation to those who eagerly await Him."[107] The essence should read that, "man is appointed to die [at least] once or should be raptured, then face judgment."

The Human Trinity

---

[105] Matthew 16:28
[106] See 1 Thessalonians 4:16-17, *supra*.
[107] Hebrews 9:27-28

A person is made of three parts from two sets of materials as illustrated above: The mundane (soil or matter) or body; the divine or breath of life; and the unique or the resultant or the soul, which is uniquely an individual: "And the LORD God formed man of the dust of the ground, and breathed into his nostrils the breath of life; and man became a living soul."[108] Thus, in man, there is both the divine and the fleshly, but the real person is the resultant, the combination of the divine and the mundane.

When a person dies, the mundane (the body) returns to dirt, the divine (the spirit) returns to God, but the uniquely individual, the soul belongs neither to the soil nor to itself, it is uniquely man, and it is kept by God for judgment. The living soul is man's DNA, one of each type for each individual, and it is that part of man that is man's real character.

The soul needs the breath of life (the spirit) to connect to God; and the mundane (the body) to exist on earth. Every human being has a part of God in them, the very part that is in tune with God and wants to worship and honor God. But every human being has flesh in them, the very part that desires the activities of the

---

[108] Genesis 2:7

flesh, such as pleasure, innovation and enterprise.

The role of the resultant man (the soul) is to manage these two natures so that, on earth, they are fruitful, and towards God, they are well-pleasing and acceptable. Thus, of the body, the Bible says, "Therefore, I urge you, brothers and sisters, in view of God's mercy, to offer your bodies as a living sacrifice, holy and pleasing to God—this is your true and proper worship."[109] But the soul of a person is the dearest (the most costly) part of a human being, and it has no reasonable value: "For the redemption of his soul is costly, and never can payment suffice."[110] There is no payment that can equitably purchase a human soul.

No wonder it cost God His own blood, His own life, to redeem the soul: "For you know that it was not with perishable things such as silver or gold that you were redeemed from the empty way of life you inherited from your forefathers, but with the precious blood of Christ, a lamb without blemish or spot."[111]

---

[109] Romans 12:1
[110] Psalm 49:8
[111] 1 Peter 1:19

It is no wonder, too, that God would do everything to save a soul: "Then Jesus told them this parable: "What man among you, if he has a hundred sheep and loses one of them, does not leave the ninety-nine in the pasture and go after the one that is lost, until he finds it?"[112] And every soul that dies, there is a homecoming party before God, because a part of God is reuniting with Him: "Precious in the sight of the LORD is the death of his faithful servants."[113]

And it is the soul of the person that is made in the image of God: "Then God said, 'Let Us make man in Our image, after Our likeness, to rule over the fish of the sea and the birds of the air, over the livestock, and over all the earth itself and every creature that crawls upon it.' So God created man in His own image; in the image of God He created him; male and female He created them."[114] The soul of a person mirrors God. Like God, it is eternal, because it cannot be recreated or de-created. Once a soul is formed, it is permanent.

---

[112] Luke 15:3-4
[113] Psalm 116:15
[114] Genesis 1:27

Christian scriptures suggest that a human being is made up of spirit, soul and body: "May God himself, the God of peace, sanctify you through and through. May your whole spirit, soul and body be kept blameless at the coming of our Lord Jesus Christ."[115] All the three parts are essential for a human being to experience life.

Daniel seems to suggest that there is a continuity of life after death: "Many of those who sleep in the dust of the ground will awake, these to everlasting life, but the others to disgrace and everlasting contempt."[116] And as noted, the present body does die and decays. What lives forever is the soul and the spirit.

When a human person dies, the body decays and becomes soil, but the spirit returns to God: "Then shall the dust return to the earth as it was: and the spirit shall return unto God who gave it."[117] The question is, what happens to the soul? In Ezekiel, God declares: "Behold, all souls are Mine; the soul of the father as well as the soul of the son is Mine. The soul who sins

---

[115] 1 Thessalonians 5:23
[116] Daniel 12:2
[117] Ecclesiastes 12:7

will die."[118] It seems very strongly suggested that the soul rests awhile before it is awaken into judgment, i.e., "who sleep in the dust of the ground will awake, these to everlasting life, but the others to disgrace and everlasting contempt."

Christian scriptures suggest that the body is the structure which houses the real person. It is christened the temple,[119] and it houses more than just the human soul; it also houses the Holy Spirit (or God Himself). The human soul, within the body is variously called: He is called the living soul: "And Jehovah God formed man of the dust of the ground, and breathed into his nostrils the breath of life; and man became *a living soul*."[120]

Other Bible versions render "a living soul" as a living being,[121] a living person,[122] a living creature,[123] a body with a spirit,[124] or a breathing man.[125] It can be inferred that a human body

---

[118] Ezekiel 18:4
[119] See 1 Corinthians 6:15-20
[120] Genesis 2:7 (American Standard Version, emphasis added)
[121] New International Version
[122] New Living Translation
[123] English Standard Version
[124] Amplified Bible
[125] See Contemporary English Version and Good News Translation

without a soul is a dead soul. It is this author's supposition that just like breath from God made man unique and responsive, when such breath returns to God in death, man becomes irresponsive until they are resurrected or raptured. However, the account of the responsive soul (which is able to both know and remember) of the rich man in torment may render this assumption problematic.[126]

What is cogent is the belief in holistic sanctification – a spiritual process in which God keeps our total man (body, soul and spirit) holy. This is both attitudinal and a gracious process as enunciated in these verses of scripture: "*Abstain* from every form of evil. *Now may the God of peace Himself sanctify you completely, and may your entire spirit, soul, and body be kept blameless at the coming of our Lord Jesus Chris*t. The One *who calls you is faithful, and He will do it.*"[127]

This passage of scriptures must be read together in the context of the human trinity and the resurrection, and it brings out four saliences. First, it is the responsibility of man to decide to abstain from evil. Man, in himself,

---

[126] See Luke 16, *supra*.
[127] 1 Thessalonians 5:22-24

can't be holy. However, he should decide to give God the place and permission to make him holy. Second, it is God who sanctifies the human spirit, soul (mind) and body after receiving the permission from man. Third, a purified or sanctified person (spirit, soul and body) is necessary to resurrection. From these verses, it can be inferred that those people whose spirits, souls and bodies were defied before or at death, would not resurrect with a divine nature, and, therefore, their destination would be Hell. And fourth, God's grace keeps the total person ready for resurrection. Just as salvation is of grace, so is resurrection. This aspect is relatable in the Subphemeral Patch.[128]

The Poetry of Creation

The Amplified version of the Bible defines a soul as "a body with a spirit."[129] This is, by far, the most correct definition of the human soul. It is the resultant creation from the marriage of the spirit (from God) and dirt (from nature). Both the spirit and dirt are eternal in nature. The spirit is divine; it can't die. The dirt (matter) does not disappear; it merely changes forms. Similarly, when matter changes from

---

[128] See chapters 2
[129] Genesis 2:7, *supra*.

one state (say liquid) to another (say gas), it does convert the energy that held the bonds in liquid to gas, and in the process it does not lose any single weight. There is a law recognized over this. It is called the Law of Conservation of Mass (LCM). LCM states that in a chemical reaction, mass is neither created nor destroyed.

Death can also be said to be the conversion of the human soul into its original materials. For, indeed, the spirit returns to God, and the body to earth where they both came from. With this hypothesis, it is now clear why death is an absolute part of life. Others would term this transformation as reincarnation, which has some probity, from matter point of view. Nevertheless, the other component that necessitates life is divine, which may make reincarnation non-articulable.

What makes the creation of the soul poetic is both the material factors and the procedure that went into it. We have established that the material factors that went into it are both divine and inexhaustible. So, the soul, in reality, is forever. The process is poetic, and even romantic. A bad soul will stay bad forever without redemption. A soul can only be defiled by sin.

Everything that God created before man were by way of a command. On Day 1, God said, "I *command* light to shine!"[130] On Day 2, God said, "I command a dome to separate the water above it from the water below it."[131] On Day 3, God said, "I command the water under the sky to come together in one place, so there will be dry ground."[132] On Day 4, God said, "I command lights to appear in the sky and to separate day from night and to show the time for seasons, special days, and years."[133] On Day 5, God said, "I command the ocean to be full of living creatures, and I command birds to fly above the earth."[134] Thus, God created everything else other than man just by a word of command. But when it came to the "making" of man, God changed His tone. God said of the making of man, "Now we will make humans, and they will be like us. We will let them rule the fish, the birds, and all other living creatures."[135]

---

[130] Genesis 1:3 (Contemporary English Version; other translations has it as "Let there be!" which still is a command (emphasis added).
[131] Ibid., verse 6
[132] Ibid., verse 7
[133] Ibid., verse 14
[134] Ibid., verse 20
[135] Ibid., verse 26

God then spends one full day, on Day 6 of creation, designing, moulding and putting man together. The tone is one of passion, just like a man and woman in love makes a baby. Then, "We will let them rule…" This is neither a job nor a command nor an assignment. It is in all scope a bequeathment, an inheritance, a gift, an endearment for perpetuity. It is a permanent statement, and in latitude, it is irrevocable. The making of a man (and woman) is informed from a passionate and familial point of view, and is motivated by love.

The structural design of a man is impeccable. Every part of it is infused with excellence: "I am fearfully and wonderfully made; Wonderful are Your works, and my *soul* knows it very well."[136] The resultant response to the handiwork of God is gratitude, joy and triumph: "For thou, LORD, hast made me *glad* through thy work: I will *triumph* in the works of thy hands."[137] And the soul of a man is the superlative of all that God ever made or created. It was, as it were, a romanticism of perfection.

The soul cannot happen without both the spirit

---

[136] Psalm 139:14 (Amplified Bible; emphasis added)
[137] Psalm 92:4-5

and the body. It is only possible under the right conditions when the two meet. God has patterned the initial creation of the soul to the continuation of creation of all living things. Taking man as an example, however the sperm of man (the spirit) is powerful, it cannot make human life without the ova (the body). The sperm needs the egg cell under the correct conditions to generate a human life. Design precedes the fusion. Just like God first spent time to work out all the details of the body in design before infusing it with the spirit to become a living soul, so does the act of procreation. The man (spirit) and the woman (body) are both necessary to procreation.

The philosophy of creation must, of necessity, entail the respect and hallowing of the divine and natural elements that come together to enable human life. The body is as important as the spirit to the resultant, unique creation known as the soul. The body is to be tendered, nourished, protected, worked out and loved and dignified (respected) from the time of birth to the time of death. Death offers the last rite of caring and honoring the body. Through it, the soul is actualized and freed to "be," as in "human be(*ing*)."

The spirit is to be watered as in reconnecting it to the Holy Spirit through praise of God, prayer, meditation and doing and being good. The spirit is the facility through which we redeem our conscience and access the heart and mind of God. The spirit, literally, creates a spiritual, divine and heavenly zone in the human being.

The resultant creation, the soul, juggles the two – the spiritual element (the spirit) and the natural element (the body). The soul is who a person is, his heart, the center of thought, character and behavior and the processor of human feelings and hub of decision-making: "For as he *thinketh* in his *heart*, so is he."[138] Here, thinking is attributed to the heart, and not to the mind. And this is only true in relation to the soul. The soul is translated "heart," and according to Jesus, those whose souls are not defiled, will be with, and see God: "Blessed are the pure in heart: for they shall see God."[139] But the soul that is defied will be lost: "The soul who sins shall die."[140] And the implication is that, a sinful soul belongs neither to the dust of the earth nor to God. Because of its

---

[138] Proverbs 23:7 (emphasis added)
[139] Matthew 5:8
[140] Ezekiel 18:20

uniqueness and components, the soul must be right with God to survive death.

The rightness of the soul is important to creation. A sinful soul defiles not only the sanctity of a person, but also endangers the purity of creation. Since this world was corrupted by the entrance of sin, God is only able to reside in the earth through pure souls. In pure souls, God re-establishes His original fellowship with humanity in the earth. Therefore, the trend of life has been towards the permanent destruction of sin, Satan and death.

Judgment in the Context of First and Second Deaths

It is not the purpose of this book to discuss Judgment Day and the aftermath. The aim of this theorem is to provide proof of what supposedly happens at death. However, it can be clearly explained how the state of death of Luke 16 fits into the doctrine of Hell and judgment with reference to two great passages in the Bible.

The proposition slated at the beginning of the discussion hypothesised that death temporarily ends all responses until the resurrection of the body. However, after careful review, especially taking Luke 16 into consideration, it was discovered that the story of Luke 16 is neither a parable nor an allegory. If Jesus was not talking about an allegory, then we are left with only one conclusion, namely, that the events of Luke 16 happened. With that conclusion, our earlier hypothesis then falls – because, at least from the perspective of the rich man, he both knew and remembered everything that happened on earth. In fact, he tried, without success, to get Abraham to send someone from "the dead" to warn his five brothers who were still alive on earth.

We also from that story learn that once the spirit leaves the human being, the soul cannot return into its body except in very few instances by miracles. Thus, no matter how torturous the abode is, the rich man was unable to escape or return to life before resurrection and judgment.

The idea of a unified judgment is sustained, notwithstanding, with reference to "tongue" and "water." In torment, the rich man thirsts and desires that Lazarus brings him water. This then would contradict the idea of a resurrected body. Unless, of course, the allusion to "tongue" and "water" is attributed to the soul, which in Hell, undergoes a cataclysmic craving for respite.

It is not clear in the passage whether Jesus is referring to the soul or the body. What is clear, though, is the fact that the rich man can feel, know and remember – and since his body was buried, according to the passage, it follows that the body is decayed leaving us with only one interpretation, namely, that Jesus was referring to the thirsty of the soul.

A body without a soul means physical death, but a soul that sins dies spiritually. Spiritual death may also mean separation from God and comfort, according to Luke 16. From these, it can be concluded, too, that, a person whose soul dies, finds themselves in torment, just like the rich man. It can also be concluded that spiritual death, like, physical death, requires the absence of the breath of life, which, according to the scriptures, returns to God.

Similarly, it is very clear in the Bible that resurrection precedes judgment. This, too, subscribes to the notion of stages in death, just as it is believed in Islam and Hinduism.

In Christianity, the stages seem to proceed within time, though one might sense that time might seem to have stopped for those in torment, and rest and comfort for the righteous might make it seem as if they have been there for eternity.

After resurrection, there will be judgment:

> "When the Son of Man comes in his glory, and all the angels with him, he will sit on his glorious throne. All the nations will be gathered before him, and he will separate the people one from another as a shepherd separates the sheep from the goats. He will put the sheep on his right and the goats on his left. "Then the King will say to those on his right, 'Come, you who are blessed by my Father; take your inheritance, the kingdom prepared for you since the creation of the world. For I was hungry and you gave me something to eat, I was thirsty and you gave me something to drink, I was a stranger and you invited me in, I needed clothes and you clothed me, I was sick and you looked after me, I was in prison and you came to visit me.' "Then the righteous will answer him, 'Lord, when did we see you

hungry and feed you, or thirsty and give you something to drink? When did we see you a stranger and invite you in, or needing clothes and clothe you? When did we see you sick or in prison and go to visit you?' "The King will reply, 'Truly I tell you, whatever you did for one of the least of these brothers and sisters of mine, you did for me.' "Then he will say to those on his left, 'Depart from me, you who are cursed, into the eternal fire prepared for the devil and his angels. For I was hungry and you gave me nothing to eat, I was thirsty and you gave me nothing to drink, I was a stranger and you did not invite me in, I needed clothes and you did not clothe me, I was sick and in prison and you did not look after me.' "They also will answer, 'Lord, when did we see you hungry or thirsty or a stranger or needing clothes or sick or in prison, and did not help you?' "He will reply, 'Truly I tell you, whatever you did not do for one of the least of these, you did not do for me.' "Then they will go away to eternal punishment, but the righteous to eternal life."[141]

---

[141] Matthew 25:41-46

The judge has been appointed; it is Jesus Christ. The criteria for endorsement is based on what may conveniently be termed a "Social Gospel." Those who did works of charity are spared, and those who did not, are damned. This passage is also validated by the teachings of other religions, such as Islam, Buddhism, Hinduism and the Chinese Taoist (and the concept of *shijie* or "release from the corpse") religions. Thus, the good that people did while they existed in the flesh matter most in judgment. The reference to "All the nations will be gathered before him [Jesus Christ]," also strongly suggests that this judgment does not respect religions. The universality of this judgment means that in every nation and order, nature has revealed what is good and right. Therefore, no-one should be able to feign ignorance or claim unfairness.

Those who did not do good deeds will be cast into Hell fire: "Depart from me, ye cursed, into everlasting fire, prepared for the devil and his angels." And, interestingly, the reference to "gnashing of teeth" may also give veracity to a bodily resurrection: "And shall cast them into a furnace of fire: there shall be wailing and gnashing of teeth."[142]

---

[142] Matthew 13:42

There is a hidden understanding here regarding the fates of Satan, demons and the lost souls. All of them cannot be completely vanished in Hell. From the available revelation, they will still remain conscious there in Hell. In a sense, Hell is more of a detention facility than an incinerator. The true and final destruction of Satan, demons and sinful souls will be in the Lake of Fire.

If the "glorious throne" judgment was a pretrial, we are told that there will also be the Great White Throne Judgment (GWTJ). And the distinction between the Matthew 25 Judgement (M25J) and the GWTJ is that in the former, both the good (sheep) and the bad (goats) appeared before Christ. However, in the GWTJ, only the goats seem to be judged. The GWTJ will take place after Christ's millennial rule, and all those who did not believe in Jesus Christ will be judged:

> Then I saw a great white throne and him who was seated on it. The earth and the heavens fled from his presence, and there was no place for them. And I saw the dead, great and small, standing before the throne, and books were opened. Another book

> was opened, which is the book of life. The dead were judged according to what they had done as recorded in the books. The sea gave up the dead that were in it, and death and Hades gave up the dead that were in them, and each person was judged according to what they had done. Then death and Hades were thrown into the lake of fire. The lake of fire is the second death. Anyone whose name was not found written in the book of life was thrown into the lake of fire.[143]

In this judgment, there is clearly the absence of the living. Death looms large. It seems like that only those who have tasted death are judged. And the assumption here is that the living and the righteous are absent. They had been resurrected in what is known as "The First Resurrection." The reason is because the righteous had been resurrected and raptured: "They came to life and reigned with Christ a thousand years. (The rest of the dead did not come to life until the thousand years were ended.)"[144] Around that time, for a thousand years, Satan remained locked up into the abyss.

---

[143] Revelation 20:11-15
[144] Revelation 20:4b and 5

There is a notable assumptive revelation related to the question and understanding of Hell. Although it was made for the devil and his angels (demons), it doesn't seem to have a deterrent effect on Satan. Moreover, if Hell would permanently end Satan's reign, there would neither be the need for the bottomless pit nor for the Lake of Fire. Hell, clearly, seems to be more of a temporary jail than a permanent prison. For lost souls, however, and since Hell was not made for them, it might seem like a permanent abode.

Everyone who will not be raptured, must taste death. However, only the righteous will experience the first resurrection: "This is the first resurrection. Blessed and holy are those who share in the first resurrection. The second death has no power over them, but they will be priests of God and of Christ and will reign with him for a thousand years."[145] The second death, which is the casting of unrighteous souls and Satan and his demons into the Lake of Fire, cannot harm those who will experience the first resurrection.

The M25J event also seems to satisfy the requirement of justice, and, in particular, of

---

[145] Ibid., verse 5b and 6

procedural fairness. In law, there is an old trite law that to be just, any legal and judicial process must allow the accused or the offender to be heard. This is known as the Right to be Heard or due process, under the old principle of Natural Justice. God (Jesus) is the ultimate judge: "But God is the Judge; He puts down one and exalts another."[146] Indeed, the Bible declares that righteousness and justice are the foundation of the Creator God's throne [God's judgment].[147] And it follows, logically, that if humans, who are evil (human), know how to give accusers opportunities to be heard, God who is good, should do so without hesitation. And He does, and will.

And one of the reasons why the souls in Hell will be subjected to M25J is because Christ would accord them their right to be heard. Thus, we note those who will be on His left asking: "'Lord, when did we see you hungry or thirsty or a stranger or needing clothes or sick or in prison, and did not help you?' He will reply, 'Truly I tell you, whatever you did not do for one of the least of these, you did not do for me.' Then they will go away to eternal punishment, but the righteous to eternal life."

---

[146] Psalm 75:7; also see Isaiah 22:33, Psalm 50:6
[147] See Psalm 89:14

In this exchange, we see that the unrighteous souls will go into eternal damnation knowing the case – the charge (accusation) and the reasons for the judgment. God is the God of justice.

It can be concluded that, the common denominator, in Christianity is, direct belief in Jesus Christ,[148] or vicariously, doing good deeds for Christ ("Social Gospel").[149] Social Gospel may be defined as the showcasing of practical faith through works of charity. Since God is not unjust,[150] it follows that even those who did not directly believe in Jesus, but if they, indirectly, did works of charity (even if they belonged to other religions), they may be spared of Hell. This is strongly suggested from the language of Matthew 25:41-46 and of Revelation 22:15. The reason why some may evade Hell through the Social Gospel is because of practical faith. James argues:

> So too, faith by itself, if it does not result in action, is dead. But someone will say, "You have faith and I have deeds." Show me your faith without deeds, and I will show you my faith

---

[148] John 3:15
[149] Matthew 25:41-46, *supra*.
[150] Hebrews 6:10

by my deeds. You believe that God is one. Good for you! Even the demons believe that—and shudder.[151]

According to James, there is living faith and dead faith. It is not enough merely to say that "I believe," it is more important to show one's belief through what they do. A person who visits the sick in hospital, prisoners in jail, gives to the poor, helps the needy or assists those who are marginalized, is engaging in practical faith, and the Maker of the universe will attribute such works to Himself. The Social Gospel meets the ends of justice by leveling the playing field, so that even the souls which might argue that they had never heard about Jesus would be fairly judged.

Sin is not only failing to believe in Jesus Christ or doing bad things (commission). Sin is, too, an omission. It can exist both as a state and a condition. All humans are presumed to be in a state of sin; they are born in sin according to the Bible: "Behold, I was brought forth in iniquity, and in sin my mother conceived me."[152]

---

[151] James 2:17-19
[152] Psalm 51:5

Sin is also a condition; people may deliberately choose to sin (disobedience): "The one who sins is the one who will die. The child will not share the guilt of the parent, nor will the parent share the guilt of the child. The righteousness of the righteous will be credited to them, and the wickedness of the wicked will be charged against them."[153]

Sin is defined in the Bible, as the transgression (violation or breaking) of the law: "Whosoever committeth sin transgresseth also the law: for sin is the transgression of the law."[154]

In short, Sin is when someone knows the good they must do but, rather, choose to do the bad or evil. The Bible mentions many varieties of sins (or works of the flesh), including: "…sexual immorality, impurity, sensuality, idolatry, sorcery, enmity, strife, jealousy, fits of anger, rivalries, dissensions, divisions, envy, drunkenness, orgies, and things like these."[155]

However, there has been a modification to the definition of Sin under the law and the one under grace. Since the resurrection of Jesus

---

[153] Ezekiel 18:20
[154] 1 John 3:4
[155] Galatians 5:19-21

Christ ushered in a new dispensation of grace (basically absence of law), Sin is no longer the breaking of the law, because there is no law to break. Under grace (a quintessential law of love), everything is permitted: "'I have the right to do anything,' you say—but not everything is beneficial. 'I have the right to do anything'—but I will not be mastered by anything."[156] Sin, therefore, is anything that is not beneficial to you and to your neighbor. If what you do or say or your attitude is not beneficial to you or your neighbor, then doing it is sin to you. Therefore, "If anyone, then, knows the good they ought to do and doesn't do it, it is sin for them." [157]

This means that, unlike in the Old Testament and in our legal systems where there was and there is a national, public deterrent system that classifies certain behaviors as wrongs (sins), under grace, such facility does not exist anymore. Sin is individualized. It is a matter of our hearts, of our consciences: "If our hearts condemn us, we know that God is greater than our hearts, and he knows everything."[158]

---

[156] 1 Corinthians 6:12
[157] James 4:17
[158] 1 John 3:20

In other words, if one's heart condemns them, they have sinned, if it doesn't, they haven't sinned. Similarly, if what one contemplates to do or say will make another person stumble, then they shouldn't do or say it. Ultimately, the only sin that takes people to Hell is because they do not or did not directly believe in Jesus or, vicariously, did not do the deeds of the Social Gospel.

Death entered the world through sin: "Therefore, just as sin entered the world through one man, and death through sin, and in this way death came to all people, because all sinned."[159] The venom of death is sin, and the strength of sin is the law: "The sting of death is sin, and the strength of sin (that is, what makes sin sting at death) is the law of God, which dooms the dying sinner to eternal punishment."[160]

Do the math: Eliminate sin, overcome death; eliminate the law, make sin weak. And God has provided the answer. First, "God made him who had no sin to be sin for us, so that in him we might become the righteousness of

---

[159] Romans 5:12
[160] 1 Corinthians 15:56

God."[161] And second, Christ instituted grace as a system of absolute vindication, no law required to be saved: "For it is by grace you have been saved, through faith—and this is not from yourselves, it is the gift of God."[162]

No wonder someone has proclaimed: "O death, where is thy sting? O grave, where is thy victory? The sting of death is sin; and the strength of sin is the law. But thanks be to God, which giveth us the victory through our Lord Jesus Christ. Therefore, my beloved brethren, be ye steadfast, unmoveable, always abounding in the work of the Lord, forasmuch as ye know that your labor is not in vain in the Lord."[163] And note here, too, triumph over death through Jesus Christ is a dual formation of faith and the Social Gospel (or good deeds motivated by love.)[164]

Conclusion

The so-called mystery of death is no longer a mystery. It is a plain reality revealed through

---

[161] 2 Corinthians 5:21
[162] Ephesians 2:8
[163] 1 Corinthians 15:55-58
[164] See Hebrews 10:24

scriptures, mental conceptions and keen observation and experience. People do die, and they don't return. Only Jesus Christ died and returned, and ascended. A few have been raised from the dead, and they died again. Whether it is from a religious or experiential point of view, humans may die once. In this chapter, we have attempted to explain the rationale for dying and not returning.

We have shown that death may suspend time, and those who die, may exist out of time, cannot breathe, and may have neither knowledge nor memory in the state of death. At resurrection, each soul will be subjected, from our point of view to judgment – some for rewards and others for condemnation – and thereafter, a new order of things will be introduced culminating in the New Jerusalem likely right here on earth. Death will be the last enemy to be destroyed, and Eternal Life will reign forever. There is some evidence, drawn from the five major religions, Hinduism, Islam, Buddhism, Taoism and Christianity, of vague stages of death. There is a strong suggestion that the soul undergoes some sort of trip before it is finally subjected to judgment. These stages, though, may contrast the thesis that death is a long silence of irresponsiveness. But whether we got it right or wrong, death does not take us by surprise, even in spontaneous accidents. God has prepared a plan of how everyone will die or be raptured. This, too, may be called grace, and is the subject of Chapter 2.

REVIEW QUESTIONS
(And Suggested Answers)

1. In your own view, how do you understand this statement: "When you have a clear view of death, you have a clear view of life."

   Answer:
   Review Chapter 1 on "The Nature of Death and Dying." Responses will vary.

2. With respect to the phrase "In a twinkling of an eye," compare sleep, death and the resurrection.

   Answer: All are expected; all happen at some point unknown.

3. What are the benefits of death from the earthly point of view?

   Answer: Rest to the body; fertilization; and regeneration

4. What does it mean that death and life are an accounting system?

   Answer:
   They must balance; what is done in life must be accounted for in the after-life; reconciliation must happen before death; life must be lived with wisdom.

5. In your own words, discuss: "Preparing for death is a lifetime's job."

   Answer:
   Responses will vary, but they include the idea that everything that is born will die; living right is implied; no-one knows when they will die, so, they ought to be prepared all the time; and etc.

6. "Death is a long silence." Identify at least two implications of this statement.

   Answer:
   Responses will vary, but the following may be suggested: Do and say rightly before death; prepare for the long sleep (put your house in order); praise and worship God before you die; and etc.

7. Compare and contrast the inspiration for death and living right among Christians, Muslims and Hindus.

   Answer:
   Responses will vary, but the review of Chapter 1 on "Human Problem, Divine Solution" may assist in the exploration of this question.

8. What are the four states of death?

Answer: Action; process; state/condition; and personality

9. In relation to power over death and life, what do the plagues of Egypt illustrate?

   Answer:
   Suggestions include – only God can create real life; Satan can kill, and so can God; witchcraft can mimic creation but it can't sustain it; Passover illustrates the ramson of blood as forerunner to the righteous blood of Jesus Christ that would be paid for the redemption of the world; and etc.

10. In regards to the "new order of things" after the resurrection and Judgment Day, there seems to be some evidence that it will be established right here on earth. Do you agree?

    Answer:
    Responses will vary. Suggestions for and against could be found in Revelation 21.

11. Fix the Hebrew 9:27 and "the-raising of the dead miracle" discrepancy.

    Answer:
    Responses will vary. Suggestions – Hebrews 9:27 stands for the one-death proposition, but those who experience the miracle of being raised from the dead eventually die twice; there is a strong indication that resurrection

for judgment will happen at the same time for everyone; and etc.

12. Discuss suicide in the context of the characteristic feature of death of the termination of the breath of life and the concept of renegation.

    Answer:
    Responses will vary. Assumptions – if only God can take a life, it may follow, therefore, that taking human life by self-killing could be viewed as murder. However, this assumption does not take into consideration the predisposition of the Patch, especially during the Subphemeral Patch in which a person might have sought for absolution and penance just before their souls renege (see Chapter 2 under "Subphemeral Resolution." Absolute judgment on this belongs to God.

13. When is abortion justified?

    Answer:
    Responses will vary. Consider factoring in the rule: "If saving the child will kill the mother, and if saving the mother will kill the child, abortion may be justified." Some may also argue that why not invoke the author of life to intervene by way of a miracle? Etc.

14. What underlies the phrase, "Death should find us empty"?

Answer: That we must fulfill our purpose before we die.

15. What are the three elements of life according to the Patch Theorem?

    Answer: Breath, knowledge or memory

16. What comes first, death or life?

    Answer:
    Responses may vary, and the debate is akin to what comes first an egg or a chicken. The idea of an empty earth becoming alive due to God's command, and the return of the spirit to God at death, may all give impetus to the debate.

17. KAD stands for ___

    Answer: Knowledge Acquisition Device

18. What does the concept of obsidousness (being obsidous) mean?

    Answer: It entails a state of being painless, irresponsive, empty and formless.

19. Name at least one example of a metaphysical craft.

    Answer: Witchcraft

20. What do we call a situation in which a person is able to breathe but can neither retain knowledge nor remember anything? Give an example.

    Answer:
    Incapacitation; coma (in some comatose situations, one may be able to retain some memory and even exercise some senses, e.g. the sense of hearing).

21. Time and death are ____ related.

    Answer: Inversely

22. What does the story of the rich man and Lazarus illustrate?

    Answer:
    Responses may vary. The central theses are that both the poor and the rich die; the soul of Lazarus (a righteous man) finds rest but that of the rich man (unrighteous man) is tortured in Hell; but the story does not imply that rich people are wicked and poor people are righteous. The story also highlights the idea of passage, time and the fact that in Hell the rich man is able to remember and to feel. But the story also seems to raise questions, such as regarding the stages in death, that death is a long silence and that the dead are unconscious.

23. Reconcile Hebrews 9:27 with the idea of a rapture.

   Answer:
   One seems to suggest that everyone will die once, the other that some may never experience death. Both may be reconciled in the resurrection, namely, that the resurrection will transform the dead into new bodies just like the ones those who will be raptured will have.

24. What is a person's DNA?

   Answer: Soul

25. The correct definition of the human soul is ___

   Answer: A body with a spirit

26. Partial Resurrection happens ___

   Answer:
   When those who are raised from the dead as a result of a miracle die again and await the final resurrection when they will face judgment.

27. How does death fit into the Law of Conservation of Mass?

   Answer:
   Death is like the conversion of the human soul into its original materials.

28. What makes the creation of the soul poetic?

    Answer:
    It is both the material factors and the procedure that went into it. The love, passion and creative design that went into the creation of the soul all point to the romanticism of perfection.

29. What should be people's attitude towards the body?

    Answer:
    The body is to be tendered, nourished, protected, worked out and loved and dignified (respected) from the time of birth to the time of death.

30. What should human beings do with the spirit?

    Answer:
    The spirit is to be watered as in reconnecting it to the Holy Spirit through the praise of God, prayer, meditation and doing and being good.

31. What is the soul?

    Answer:
    The resultant creation, the soul, juggles the two – the spiritual element (the spirit) and the natural element (the body). The soul is who a person is, his heart, the center of thought,

character and behavior and the processor of human feeling and the hub of decision-making.

32. What kills the soul and gives death its lethal bite?

    Answer: **Sin**

33. What is Christianity's foremost doctrine?

    Answer: The resurrection

34. Distinguish between the Great White Throne Judgment (GWTJ) and the Matthew 25 Judgement (M25J)?

    Answer:
    During the GWTJ only goats (the bad) are judged. During M25J goats (the bad) are separated from sheep (the good).

35. What is the Social Gospel?

    Answer: It is the showcasing of practical faith through works of charity.

36. What is the definition of Sin under the doctrine of grace?

    Answer:
    It is contained in this statement, "If anyone, then, knows the good they ought to do and doesn't do it, it is sin for them."

37. What makes Sin strong?

    Answer: The law

38. What is common between the Old Testament and our criminal legal systems?

    Answer: They are both considered to be a national, public deterrent and punitive system.

39. Grace is quintessentially a ___

    Answer: Law of love

40. Who has the power to defeat death?

    Answer: Jesus Christ, and those who put their trust in Him.

41. BOLE stands for ___

    Answer: Breath of Life Exchange

42. What justifies God's justice pursuant to M25J?

    Answer:
    Procedural Fairness or the Right to be Heard

2 | THE PATCH

Chapter Content

The Soul's Delicate Design
The Subconscious Patch
The Subcortical Patch
The Subphemeral Patch
Conclusion

The Soul's Delicate Design

As discussed in Chapter 1, the soul is the center of human impulse, the partly-God and partly-nature man. The soul is eternal and it defaults towards right. Due to the layered forces that impact upon it, including temptations, desires, ambitions, and fleshly influences, it tends to be wrapped into a Cocoon of Obsequiousness (COO). The strength of COO is evil. The soul, however, is made with the capacity to know God. This facility, let us call it, the First Requisite Faith (or FRF), informs one of the existence of an invisible God.[165] It begins, in the Subconscious

---

[165] See Hebrews 11:1, 6

Patch, by analyzing God, asking such rudimentary questions as why doesn't God appear in human form, is God a man or woman, who made God, does God die, does God have a body and mind, and similarly-situated queries. But as the soul navigates the Subconscious Patch and into the Subcortical Patch and beyond, the soul sort of, becomes settled and the question of whether there is a God is infinitely rested into it. That is why the Christian Bible says that only fools say that there is no God.[166] Because being aware of the existence of God is imbedded in the soul's DNA.

It doesn't take FRF much time to quickly drown COO. In some people, especially in those who are exposed to religion earlier, this might happen even during the Subconscious Patch. Despite the early resolution of the FRF, it, however, may take a lifetime to overcome COO in other areas. For the most part, the soul ends up being a servant of COO.

As a servant of the COO, the soul finds itself doing the things that it knows to be contrary to good and God. It is then left languishing into

---

[166] See Psalm 14:1

the quandary of servitude, where it should be freed to return to its true nature of righteousness and freedom. Within the soul, is an in-built facility we may call The Patch, which is like an internal alarm clock towards death. It ticks less the far away a person is from death, and gets it louder the closer they are to death. The Patch system seems to be divided into three parts: The Subconscious Patch; the Subcortical Patch; and the Subphemeral Patch. These three are collectively known as the Triphemeral Dimensions of the Patch (TDP).

(1) The Subconscious Patch

The first Patch is an innocuous one, termed the "Subconscious Patch" – the pre-born, babies and toddlers belong here. It is an amazingly enjoyable patch. Everything is taken care of by nature and fate. There is no social, spiritual, economic, or financial concern. The only concern is physical (the safety of the body). The brain (mind) is in its formidable stage; it is a *tabula rasa*; anything can be written on it.

The heart is the chief center of the system, it subconsciously powers needs and their resolutions. Nature and fate have already provided the safenets of a social nature, such as parents, siblings or even governmental social services. This patch lasts until one is around seven or eight years of age. Within the TDP, the Subconscious Patch may be characterized by the following:

From Pre-birth to After-birth

This is the highest level of innocence and the tenderest and the earliest stage in the soul development. In this stage, it is more spirit than body, and it tends, naturally, to leaning towards good and God. KAD is actively developing, but knowledge and memory have not developed fully. In this stage, infancy is the job description and truth is currency.

Dependent Stage

The child depends wholly on others, and by extension, on God. At this stage, too, the Filial Inclination Mechanism (FIM), which reaches its decline within the soul during the Subcortical Patch, tends to be nimble and more perceptive and is strongest. FIM is loudest during this stage of the TDP. FIM is stronger during the Subcortical Patch and is weakest during the Subphemeral Patch. People's FIM weakens as they grow older, partly because they are themselves preparing to be parents.

The characteristics of FIM include sensitivity towards infancy; exhorted care; love for life and distaste for death; and *tenderization* (the ability to feel empathy and to make unconditional sacrifices for the benefit of the infant).

The Milk Stage of Life

The Subconscious Patch is the milk stage of life. It is wired to survive on one product, milk. In it, it finds all the nutrients it needs for bone, muscle and blood formation. Milk alone is able to sustain its life. Milk is the food of the soul. It is responsible for soul strengthening and versatility.

From the beginning, God recommended milk, even where there was lack of food. Milk, generally, is a great source of protein, calcium, and calories for growing children,[167] and so on. Accordingly:

> Breast milk contains a unique mix of
> fatty acids, lactose, amino acids,

---

[167] Carol DerSarkissian, "What to Know About Cow's Milk for Babies," WebMD, May 26th, 2021

> vitamins, minerals, enzymes, and other important factors that combine to make the perfect infant food. It has everything a baby needs for easy digestion, brain development, and protection from illness and infections.[168]

It is no accident that in their formidable stages, babies develop well when breastfed. It is because God has put everything the soul needs to develop well in milk. Apart from calcium, milk also contains tryptophan, which promotes the release of serotonin, and serotonin is good for the brain.

Honey, on the other hand, is the food of the body. The sweetness of honey represents delight and joy. Milk is necessary to fertility, honey to vitality. Honey is the most natural sweetener in the world and is also a healthy addition to many desserts and breakfasts. Honey contains tryptophan and potassium, which in that combination actively reduces anxious feelings and helps the body to relax; it also reduces stress.

---

[168] Mottchildren.org, "Feeding Your Baby and Toddler (Birth to Age Two)," https://www.mottchildren.org/posts/your-child/feeding-your-baby-toddler#breastfeeding accessed on August 3rd, 2022

God has always balanced this approach in His parenting of the souls of the human race. God recommended milk and honey to everyone, not only to children. It is because milk and honey are necessary to the continued development of the soul and the body, respectively. When He delivered the Israelites from Egypt, he recommended milk (for the soul) and honey (for the body): "So, I have come down to deliver them from the power of the Egyptians, and to bring them up from that land to a good and spacious land, to a land flowing with milk and honey…"[169] A person needs milk at the Subconscious Patch more than at any other stage of the TDP.

Pleasure-seeking Development Stage

Pleasure is a quality first found in God: "God saw all that he had made, and *it was very good.*"[170] And God also desires that He is man's source of delight and pleasure: "Take delight in the LORD, and he will give you the desires of your heart [soul]."[171] It is simple: Pleasure yourself

---

[169] Exodus 3:8a; see also Numbers 13:27, Deuteronomy 6:3, Joshua 5:6, Jeremiah 11:5, Job 20:17, etc.
[170] Genesis 1:31 (emphasis added)
[171] Psalm 37:4

in God; He will also ensure your pleasure. What we call pleasing God, is nothing other than giving God all the pleasure.

God primarily has called all human beings to praise and worship Him: "It is written: 'Worship the Lord your God and serve him only.'"[172] Praise and worship are acts of pleasure – delight, adoration and affirmation. God not only seeks for true worshippers, but He also demands it: "Yet a time is coming and has now come when the true worshipers will worship the Father in the Spirit and in truth, for they are the kind of worshipers the Father seeks."[173] And the culminating verse is, "Let everything that has breath praise the LORD."[174]

Very young children love pleasure because their souls are closer to God than to the polluted world. Here is a fundamental truth. The Pleasure Seeking Mechanism (PSM) in children is pure, unadulterated and genuine. It longs for love, comfort and endearing. The PSM in children is so strong that they cry if pleasure is not being met. Adults sometimes

---

[172] Luke 4:8
[173] John 4:23
[174] Psalm 150:6

tend to construe this as intrusion or childishness or imprisoning. PSM is weaker in adults because their souls tend to give in to temptations for selfishness, greed, egotism and self-love.

PSM is pure, unselfish (though adults may try to interpret the soul of children's pressure-seeking tendencies as selfishness. Their PSM is divine, motivated by the need to fulfill the God-like energy that leads to higher praise), and godly. The Bible is clear on this: "For men [and women] will be *lovers of themselves*, lovers of money, boastful, arrogant, abusive, disobedient to their parents, ungrateful, unholy, unloving, unforgiving, slanderous, without self-control, brutal, *without love of good*, traitorous, reckless, conceited, *lovers of pleasure rather than lovers of God*."[175] The lynchpin of these verses is love for self rather than love for God.

When PSM begins to be fogged by greed, lust and other vices in adulthood, the soul begins to retreat and the flesh starts to dominate. That's when pleasure is hijacked by lust and becomes corrupted. Uncontrolled pleasure for fleshly desires leads to the death of the soul. But channeling pleasure to the praise and honor of

---

[175] 2 Timothy 3:2-4

God uplifts the human soul – bringing it even closer to God. Whether they know it or not, PSM lingers in humans for their entire life; those who don't use it for the praise and worship of God, use it for selfish desires or for the praise and worship of idols (anything that takes the place of God in one's life).

(2) The Subcortical Patch

Emotional Restructuring Experience

The Subcortical Patch is the second stage of the TDP. It is crucial because of what may be termed as the Emotional Restructuring Experience (or ERE). ERE involves the complex activities such as memory, emotion, pleasure and hormone production. Under the Subconscious Patch, these were present and they were in their purest state. If uncorrupted, souls would continue to be pure. They express themselves in the form of pleasure-seeking and by what may be termed as Truth-in-Emotions or TIE. TIE, like PSM, is strongest during the Subconscious Patch. It is inhibited during the Subcortical Patch.

Truth-in-Emotions

ERE imposes itself on TIE in its quest to safeguard the soul. Inhibition of TIE leads to experiencing life informed by lies and untruths. People no longer express their pure, basic instinct and emotions because they are ashamed or too conscious of who they are or because they do not want to offend the core culture, and so on. In short, their emotional experience is more fake than original; it has been modified from its original place of purity and truthfulness. Therefore, a smile may not be a smile anymore, laughter may be distress, and saying "yes" may mean saying "no."

As can be expected, during the Subcortical Patch, the soul is in distress. It is working on shading off what is called the *Corrugated Experience* (an experience in which the soul's voice is relegated to that of the body, and in which the soul struggles to regain its God-like character) brought about by ERE in order to reclaim TIE, leading to the Resolution. Otherwise, it leads to damnation. This is simplified in the following formulas:

$$\text{TIE} > \text{ERE} = \text{"R"}$$
(where "R" is the resolution)

and

$$\text{TIE} < \text{ERE or ERE} > \text{TIE} = \text{"D"}$$
(where "D" is damnation)

The Resolution

TIE and the Resolution are related. The Resolution is the state of the human being where the soul is freed to live up to truth. Most people reach the Resolution at the mouth of death. Some don't. What is called death confessions are, many times, simply the Resolution reached and expiated. It comes about because TIE has triumphed over ERE. Although this may happen during the Subcortical Patch; it more often than not happens during the Subphemeral Patch.

The Resolution has the witness of the three members of the Trimodular of Human Structuration (or THS): Spirit, soul and body. The Resolution is conscious, and it may include repentance, confession and absolution. The Resolution may also happen because of fear –

such as when a person fears to go to Hell and makes their "life right before God." It can also happen because of love – such as when the Gospel is preached and the message of love overcomes ERE and releases the soul into accepting the way of salvation.

The Resolution may be formulaic such as through *shahada* in Islam or altar-call in Christianity (also known as saying the sinners' prayer). The love motivated Resolution is the strongest because it does not fade even when the circumstances change, such as if the person ends up living if they were about to die, or if the source of fear is eliminated or if Hell is not that frightening any more.

So, from as early as seven years old, to as later as 70 years of age, one has entered into the Subcortical Patch. It is the most consequential patch; the final resolution (what is called the Subphemeral Resolution)[176] may depend on it.

The Equilibrium

During the Subcortical Patch, the undeveloped

---

[176] This is different from the Resolution of the Subcortical Patch; the Subphemeral Resolution happens during the Subphemeral Patch.

brain (mind) has gotten shape, and the heart is strong and agile. The emotional center is functioning per maximus. Strength is generated in massive amounts and the ultimate composition of the THS, which is simply another way of saying the soul, body and spirit, should be in balance. The ultimate objective of this Patch is the use of personal judgment in making decisions that are both humane and divine.

Assumptions of the Subcortical Patch

With a balanced THS (THS in equilibrium), the following assumptions may be drawn:

1. One has already resolved the Subconscious Patch; THS is in equilibrium;
2. One no longer lives for themselves; they realize that they are part of God and part of the human race;
3. The body isn't the only structure developed; the spirit and soul have been mortally refined;
4. The two other members of the THS (soul and spirit) are being tenderized within TIE; and
5. One is presumed to understand the

intricacy of cause and effect, morality and immorality, responsibility and carelessness, action and inaction, love and hate, good and bad and right and wrong.

Any upset in the assumptions may affect the Resolution, and ultimately, if it is not resolved by the Subphemeral Resolution, it may compromise the soul for eternity.

(3) The Subphemeral Patch

The Christian Bible illustrates the fate of the last state of TDP in this verse: "[As for] the days of our years, in them are seventy years; and if [men should be] in strength, eighty years; and the greater part of them would be labor and trouble; for weakness overtakes us, and we shall be chastened."[177]

The first Resolution is expected to happen during the Subcortical Patch. But it may not. And as humans make transition into their seventies and post-seventies, TIE has pretty much conquered ERE and for many, this is the stage in which they feel more comfortable to

---

[177] Psalm 90:10

commit their souls to God in preparation for death. For others, even in their seventies or post-seventies, they may still be struggling with doubts, unbelief or bad habits.

However, in their seventies, God and nature combined provide another layer, Christians may call this grace, that may enable them to transition into the after-life with less struggle. The *Grace Configuration* of the Subphemeral Patch consists of the following which impact upon the THS (soul, body and spirit): The Subphemeral Consciousness; the Subphemeral Deconfrigration; and the most consequential, the Subphemeral Resolution.

Subphemeral Consciousness

At this stage of Subphemeral Patch in the TDP, the soul should have a larger voice than the body. For many people, their bodies are in a state of pain and weakness. However, their soul is strong and is ready, if required, to be united with God. The spirit is ever ready and in combination, the soul and the spirit make the person more conscious of the after-life and of God than before this stage.

Subphemeral Deconfrigration

And systematically, but unconsciously, a person is able to reach clear-cut conclusions about their own life and the life after-death. Even if the person was irreligious, somehow unconsciously they may come to a conclusion that there is a Hell and a Heaven. They will also begin to understand the implication of their own state of being. TIE is liberated.

This, which is now called the Subphemeral Deconfrigration, is only possible because of the Subphemeral Consciousness. Because of this very clear-cut awareness of their conditions, people at this stage may also become aware of their true destination. Unlike at the Resolution during the Subcortical Patch of the TDP, here at this stage, the soul, if inundated by sins, desires absolution, and, if it had reached absolution, it would be ready to be accepted by God.

Subphemeral Resolution

The Subphemeral Resolution is the ultimate point at which the person's soul either enters into eternal peace with God or where, if missed, a person's soul becomes a prisoner unto destruction. It's possible, as postulated by some religions, that a person can experience purgatorial grace through the prayers of those left behind. However, Subphemeral Resolution doesn't happen before the dissembling of the THS.

A person is at the border between life and death, which, in THS parlance, is construed as that they still have breath, or they know and remember, and, therefore, they are alive. At this stage, only their own prayers for penance and absolution can save them from Hell. As long as the spirit still inhabits the body, there is hope of the resolution unto salvation of the soul. Otherwise, prayers (uttered, vocalized or silent within) may be of little or no effect on the redemption of the soul once breath ceases and the soul reneges (*renegation* is the revocation of the soul by God). Once renegation happens, the body can only be returned to the earth and the soul either awaits Hell or is kept to rest.

Conclusion

The TDP is a facility of grace, affixed by divinity and nature to save the soul from eternal damnation. Hence, the Subphemeral Resolution, especially, shows that, even in unlikely and impossible situations, God has given humans a chance to save the soul. Those who ignore or dance around it, do so to their own peril, and do harm to their own eternal destination. In the Bible, it is revealed in this verse: "God is not willing that any should perish, but that all should come to repentance."[178] The plain fact is that the Subphemeral Resolution can happen in split milliseconds, because every soul in a person wishes to be in the presence of its Maker.

---

[178] 2 Peter 3:9

REVIEW QUESTIONS
(With Suggested Answers)

1. COO stands for ___

   Answer: Cocoon of Obsequiousness

2. When is TIE said to be at liberty?

   Answer:
   It is during the Subphemeral Deconfrigration.

3. What do we collectively call the three divisions of the Patch?

   Answer:
   The Triphemeral Dimensions of the Patch or TDP

4. The three Patches are ___

   Answer:
   The Subconscious Patch; the Subcortical Patch; and the Subphemeral Patch

5. To what Patch do the pre-born, babies and toddlers belong?

   Answer: The Subconscious Patch

6. List the three characteristic stages of the Subconscious Patch:

   Answer:
   From pre-birth to after-birth – dependent stage; the milk stage of life; pleasure-seeking development stage;

7. What does FIM stand for?

   Answer: Filial Inclination Mechanism

8. What are the main characteristics of FIM?

   Answer:
   Sensitivity towards infancy; exhorted care; love for life and distaste for death; and tenderization.

9. Define tenderization.

   Answer:
   The ability to feel empathy and to make unconditional sacrifices for the benefit of the infant.

10. Why is milk also known as the food of the soul?

    Answer: Because it is by itself able to sustain life.

11. If milk is necessary to fertility, honey is to ___

Answer: Vitality

12. Where is the pleasure quality first found?

    Answer: In God.

13. Name three components of pleasure.

    Answer:
    Delight, adoration and affirmation.

14. Name two acts of pleasure.

    Answer: Praise and worship

15. What does PSM stand for?

    Answer: Pleasure Seeking Mechanism

16. When is PSM strongest and weakest?

    Answer:
    It is strongest in children and weakest in adults.

17. What does PSM long for?

    Answer: Love, comfort and endearing.

18. Where does the God-like energy lead?

    Answer: To higher praise.

19. What fogs PSM?

    Answer:
    Greed, lust and other vices in adulthood.

20. What is PSM's lifespan?

    Answer: Till death.

21. What does ERE stand for?

    Answer:
    Emotional Restructuring Experience.

22. Where is ERE situated?

    Answer: In the Subcortical Patch.

23. What does the ERE involve?

    Answer:
    It involves the complex activities such as memory, emotion, pleasure and hormone production.

24. What does TIE stand for?

    Answer: Truth-in-Emotions

25. What is Corrugated Experience?

Answer:
It is an experience in which the soul's voice is relegated to that of the body.

26. State the formula in which ERE and TIE interact leading to Resolution.

Answer:

$$TIE > ERE = \text{``R''}$$
(where "R" is the resolution)

27. State the formula in which ERE and TIE interact leading to a Damnation.

Answer:

$$TIE < ERE \text{ or } ERE > TIE = \text{``D''}$$
(where "D" is the damnation)

28. What is a Resolution?

Answer:
It is the state of the human being during the Subcortical Patch where the soul is freed to live up to truth.

29. What does THS stand for?

Answer: Trimodular of Human Structuration

30. What is the ultimate objective of the Subphemeral Patch?

Answer:
It is the use of personal judgment in making decisions that are both humane and divine.

31. A balanced THS is also called ___

    Answer: Equilibrium

32. How many assumptions does the Subcortical Patch have, and what is affected if there is any upset in the assumptions?

    Answer: Five (5); the Resolution

33. Name the constituent parts of the Grace Configuration of the Subphemeral Patch.

    Answer:
    The Subphemeral Consciousness; the Subphemeral Deconfrigration; and Subphemeral Resolution.

34. At what stage do most people become aware of their true spiritual destination?

    Answer: Subphemeral Deconfrigration

35. What is the ultimate point at which the person's soul either enters into eternal peace with God or where, if missed, a

person's soul becomes a prisoner unto destruction?

Answer: The Subphemeral Resolution

36. The evidence that the soul of a person is wired to know God is a facility known as ___

    Answer: First Requisite Faith (or FRF)

37. Is there evidence to suggest that FRF is predisposed to suppressing COO?

    Answer: Yes

38. According to the Bible, what is ultimate foolishness?

    Answer:
    An assertion that there is no God

39. What is faith?

    Answer:
    The substance of things hoped for or the evidence of things not seen.

40. What do we call the internal alarm system designed by divinity and nature to alert the human soul against death; and what conceptual term is associated with it?

    Answer: The Patch; grace

ABOUT THE AUTHOR

Charles Mwewa (LLB; BA. Education; BA. Legal Studies; Cert. Law; DIBM; LLM Cand.) is a Dad, author, lawyer, educator, and moral and social influencer. Mwewa is the author of 30 books and counting in all genres – fiction (novels), non-fiction and poetry. Mwewa, his wife, and their three girls, reside in the Capital City of Ottawa, Canada.

INDEX

A

Abel, 13
Abortion. *See* Suicide
Abraham, 45
absolution, 67, 130, 135, 136
accusation. *See* charge
Adam and Eve. *See* Garden of Eden
after-life, 6, 8, 40
Alfred Russel. *See* Evolution Theory
Allah, 6, 42, 53, 55, 56, 57, 58
amino acids. *See* milk stage of life
Apostle Paul, 11, 46
asleep. *See* sleep

B

baptism, 14
benefits, 3, 44
Bible, 13, 43, 44, 47, 48, 50, 52
blood formation. *See* milk stage of life
BOLE. *See* Breath of Life Exchange, *See* Breath of Life Exchange
bone. *See* milk stage of life
brain. *See* mind
brain development. *See* milk stage of life
breath of life, 20, 28, 30, 31, 32
Breath of Life Exchange, 33
Buddhism, 8

C

Cain. *See* Abel
calcium. *See* milk stage of life
calories. *See* milk stage of life
Canada, 147
caring, 25, 51
cemetery, 22
character, 25, 40
charge, 100
Charles Darwin. *See* Evolution Theory
cherubim. *See* Garden of Eden
chicken. *See* egg
children, 5, 11
Christianity, 8, 9, 44, 46, 47,

52, 53
coma, 31
comatose. *See* coma
condemn, 39
Confucius, 6, 8
conscience, 13
consciousness, 39, 43
Creationist Theory., vii
Creator, 2, 3, 13, 23, 28

empty, 24
enzymes. *See* milk stage of life
equalizer, 2
equilibrium. *See* THS
Eternal Life, 12, 106
evidence, 57, 106
Evolution Theory. *See* Creationist Theory

D

David, 24
Day of Judgement. *See* Judgment Day
Day of Resurrection, 42
Death and Hades, 9
decay, 27
discretion, 53, 57, *See* BOLE
diseases, 32
dispensation, 1
dreaming. *See* sleep
due process. *See* Natural Justice

F

faculties, 26
fatty acids. *See* milk stage of life
fear, 5, 12, 22, 51
fertilization. *See* benefits
Filial Inclination Mechanism, 122
FIM. *See* Filial Inclination Mechanism
First Requisite Faith, 119
fool, 25
form, 27
FRF. *See* First Requisite Faith
fruitless life, 12

E

earth, 3, 12, 15, 16, 22, 23, 24, 25, 28, 29, 32, 44, 48, 49
easy digestion. *See* milk stage of life
egg, 26
Egypt. *See* Moses
elements, 20, 39, 53

G

Garden of Eden, 60
generations, 11, 24, 26
glory, 10, 25
God's will. *See* discretion
God's Word, 28
God-like energy. *See*

Pleasure Seeking Mechanism
grace, 52
greatness, 4

H

Hades. *See* Hell
hallucination, 31
Heaven, 9, 12, 48
Hebrews, 15, 43, 44, 45, 47
Hell, 4, 9, 45, 49
Holy City. *See* New Jerusalem
honey, 124, 125

I

incapacitation, 30, 31, 32
incarnation, 9, 40, 41, 42
infant. *See* tenderization
Islam. *See* Allah

J

Jahannam. *See* Hell
Jesus Christ, 8, 9, 10, 11, 14, 106
John Milton. *See* Paradise Lost
Joseph, 10
Judaism, 52, *See* Sabbath
Judgment Day, 4, 8, 39
justice. *See* Natural Justice

K

KAD. *See* Knowledge Acquisition Device
Karma, 8
knowledge, 20, 26, 29, 30, 32, 39, 43, 106
Knowledge Acquisition Device, 29

L

Lake of Fire. *See* second death
Law of Conservation of Mass, 85
Lazarus, 45
LCM. *See* Law of Conservation of Mass
life-support, 31
live baby, 27

M

magicians. *See* Moses
memories, 22, 23
memory, 20, 26, 29, 30, 32, 39, 42, 43, 106, 128
milk stage of life, 123
mind, 121
minerals. *See* milk stage of life
mortals, 38
Moses, 16, 19, 48, 49
Muhammad. *See* Allah

muscle. *See* milk stage of life
Muslims, 8, 42, 43, 46, 53
mystery, 26, 105

N

Natural Justice, 99
natural sweetener. *See* honey
New Jerusalem, 61

O

observation. *See* obsidous, 30

P

painless, 30
paradise, 40
Paradise. *See* Garden of Eden
Paradise Lost, 60
Passover, 19
Patch, 121
penance, 136
perception, 26
personality, 13
Peter, 5, 9, 10
Pharaoh. *See* Moses
plague. *See* Moses
pleasure. *See* Pleasure Seeking Mechanism
Pleasure Seeking Mechanism, 126
poisons, 14
potassium. *See* honey
prayer, 12
prejudicial effect. *See* evidence
probative value. *See* evidence
procedural fairness. *See* Natural Justice
protein. *See* milk stage of life
providence, 23
PSM. *See* Pleasure Seeking Mechanism
punishment, 20

R

reduces stress. *See* honey
refinement, 3
regeneration. *See* benefits
reincarnation, 41
renegation, 136
reneges. *See* renegation
resurrection, 2, 4, 8, 9, 12, 14, 32, 39, 40, 41, 42, 45, 46, 47, 50, 52, 106
revocation. *See* renegation
Right to be Heard. *See* Natural Justice
righteousness, 12, *See* Natural Justice

S

Sabbath, 49
salvation, 10, 52, 53
Satan, 11, 16, 19
Saturday. *See* Sabbath, *See* Sabbath
scholars, 44
second death, 14, 51
serotonin. *See* milk stage of life
Seventh Day Adventists. *See* Sabbath
shahada. See Shariah Law
Shariah Law, 53
sleep, 2, 5, 8, 39
Social Gospel, 95, 100, 104, 105
soul, 3, 7, 11, 22, 27, 43, 106
Spirit. *See* God's Word
subconscious, viii, x, 39
Subconscious Patch. *See* Patch
subcortical, 53
Subcortical Patch, 128, *See* Patch
subphemeral, viii, 53
Subphemeral Consciousness, 134
Subphemeral Deconfrigration, 134
Subphemeral Patch, 133
Subphemeral Resolution, 134
substance. *See* form

Suicide, 20
sweetness. *See* honey

T

TDP, 122
temporary death, 32
tenancy. *See* BOLE
tenderization, 123
thief. *See* Satan
THS. *See* trimodular of human structuration, *See* Trimodular of Human Structuration
Tree of Knowledge of Good and Evil. *See* Garden of Eden
Tree of Life. *See* Garden of Eden
trimodular of human structuration, 53
tryptophan. *See* milk stage of life

U

unborn, 20
unconditional sacrifices. *See* tenderization
unrighteousness. *See* righteousness

V

vision, 5, 24

vitality. *See* honey
vitamins. *See* milk stage of
  life

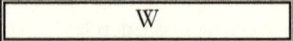

W

wealth, 23, 25

wisdom, 5
witchcraft, 32
Word of God, ix
worm, 51

www.ingramcontent.com/pod-product-compliance
Lightning Source LLC
Chambersburg PA
CBHW032120040426
42449CB00005B/201

9781988251417